To Elizabeth
– with thanks
God bless
Eric Stenway
16/12/07

From Brickbats to Bouquets

Published by Lonely Scribe
www.lonelyscribe.co.uk

First published 2007

Copyright © Eric Stanway 2007

Cover design and typesetting
copyright © Armadillo Design Ltd 2007

ISBN: 978-1-905179-03-9

From Brickbats to Bouquets

Kingswood Approved School
1955 – 1957

Eric Stanway

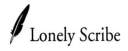 Lonely Scribe

For Joyce, my wife,

who gave me steadfast support

and love when things were

at their most difficult

Methodist Relief &
Development Fund

*In Joyce's memory, all royalties from
the sale of this book are donated to the
Methodist Relief and Development Fund,
of which she was an enthusiastic supporter*

Contents

Foreword

This is an intriguing book about boys – disturbed, difficult and sometimes dangerous boys – and how their care had a deep impact upon a couple drawn into the work of what were then approved schools. It centres upon the 1950s and 1960s when there was little careful insight into the many ways in which boys can become thus disturbed, little detailed knowledge of autism, post-traumatic stress disorder, dyslexia, and so on, and therefore little awareness of appropriate treatments. And yet, and yet... it is the story of how intuition, concern, listening, caring, hoping, can unlock many a disturbed boy's secrets and troubles. And so Eric and Joyce discovered their joint calling.

It is an unusual but gripping story, full of failures and successes and of the strains and stresses endured by their marriage as both of them struggled to go on caring and learning. It is told with remarkable honesty, which makes it so much more valuable. It is also at times very funny, full of ironies and wry smiles. At the end, one finds oneself being so deeply thankful that couples like this devoted their lives in a deliberate and at times immensely costly way to bother with other people's damaged children. But then, Eric and Joyce Stanway were no ordinary couple.

I met them through the Methodist church in Dursley, Gloucestershire, when invited there for a weekend. It had been my parents' home church, in which I had been baptised, a community to which the Stanways were giving rich leadership and offering warm hospitality to visitors like me and my wife (and later some of our children too). We realised at once that this vibrant couple had had a remarkable career in the service of 'delinquent' boys, with Eric having been an outstanding head of a Special School, but by this time he had been caught up in local politics as a district councillor, in a huge range of local interests and issues, and in support of one of their daughters, living just up the road, who had acquired a family of no fewer than fifteen children. She must be, one might say, 'a chip off the old block'.

So, it is a privilege to proffer this foreword. I should add that there is one particular refrain which also runs through the book. It concerns the deep Christian faith into which Eric and Joyce were reared and to which they were wholly committed. The book never, as it were, protrudes this faith, and yet one can sense it undergirding the whole account. It helped sustain their conviction of the total worthwhileness of their work, their belief that despite all the damages those boys had sustained there was still in every one a hungry soul longing for love and capable of redemption. This book is something of a shout of confidence in humanity, and in tough, discerning love. And so it shows how, in premises originally built by their beloved John Wesley, the rebuilding of young lives was still going on. A good read indeed.

Richard Jones
Former President of the Methodist Conference
and former Chair of MRDF
July 2007

CHAPTER 1

Early days

"Sit down boys, my name's Stanway, give me your names for a seating plan so that I can get to know you."

"Tony Brown." "John Smith." "Gary Thompson." "Robert Davies." So far so good, then the rot set in.

"Adolf Hitler." "Tarzan." "Mickey Mouse." All accompanied by a sudden and increasingly noisy outbreak of shuffling feet, coughing and derisive laughter.

I should have been prepared for anything after three and a half years in the army and eight years as a secondary modern teacher in a Derbyshire mining area. But with this group of twenty-four fifteen- to sixteen-year-old delinquents in an approved school, condemned to spend a day in a classroom doing 'academic' work instead of the carpentry, stonemasonry, painting and decorating or gardening they much preferred, I suddenly realised that I was in a different world. The situation was made much worse by the fact that there had been a six month gap between my accepting the appointment at Kingswood Training School and taking it up. During that time the hated schoolroom work had been non-existent. I was now the focus of the mob's discontent, the instrument of their punishment. I was overwhelmed by a sense of impending disaster. I rapidly ran through my repertoire of parlour tricks: pained silence, tactical ignoring, fierce expression, close proximity to the imagined ring leaders and so on – all to no effect. Finally, a parade ground roar bought an uneasy silence.

"Right, you've had your bit of fun. Now we'll start work."

If only I had listened to my esteemed and experienced colleague, my next-door neighbour both at home and in the classroom, who had tried to prepare me for what I could expect on that fateful Wednesday. "Have the work for the day ready and waiting on the tables," he had counselled. "Have pencils, pens and rulers set out and, whatever you do, don't give them time to think before they start work."

I was prepared, but the books, worksheets, textbooks and writing equipment were lurking in neat piles in the cupboard behind me! In the comparative hush following my bellow I turned to open the cupboard and half a brick whizzed past my ear and smashed a hole in the door. At least this brought a deathly hush while my tormentors waited to see what retribution I could conjure up. If only I could think of some adequate response but I dredged through my eight years of teaching experience and came up with nothing but imminent doom. I made some inane remark along the lines of "Someone's dropped a brick." Suddenly five o'clock, the end of the school day at Kingswood, seemed a very long way off and my previous school a distant oasis of peace.

My humiliation was completed an hour or so later when I had to be rescued from a confrontation with a towering sixteen-year-old by the deputy head. The youngster had been totally and, as I recognised later, justifiably frustrated at his inability to tackle the comprehension exercise I had set him. Simple as it was, it required a minimum reading skill he had not yet acquired. Desk, books, inkpot and all went flying in an flurry of rage and expletives.

Somehow or another this most disastrous day of my whole teaching career ground to a halt and I metaphorically limped round the massive main school building and down the drive to our new home near the school entrance. Home to a loving wife and two small daughters who had spent a day exploring their new surroundings and finding everything fresh and exciting.

"What sort of a day have you had dear?"

"A few excitements but not too bad on the whole."

This pathetic lie did not deceive for long. Three days at Kingswood had already reduced me to a pale shadow of the confident teacher I had been previously, and soon I was pouring out the whole sad story of a miserable day. Too sick at heart to eat the meal she had prepared I sat in mute misery while she, had I but known it in my selfish absorption with my own problems, covered up her own homesickness and her struggle to come to terms with a new, and suddenly frightening, future. More resilient than me, she set about boosting my shattered ego and giving me new courage to go on. Not that we had any choice. We had sold the delightful house we had built, under the licence necessary in those years, had optimistically invested the modest profits we had made in a new Ford Popular car and were now in rented accommodation tied to the job. Why, oh why had we burned our boats with such a disastrous step?

My thoughts went back wistfully to the secondary modern school in Derbyshire where I had started teaching in January 1947 and which now seemed like a haven of tranquillity compared with my present situation. Of course when one looks back it is easy to forget one's first difficulties…

. . . . .

When I first started at Alfreton Secondary Modern, newly married and fresh from teacher training college, the headmaster, Mr Dawes, popularly know as Winky for reasons I never understood and certainly never questioned, made it clear that I was in a privileged position. I was to have as my special responsibility Form 1A. First year A-stream boys! I was responsible for their Mathematics and English as well as my own specialisms of Geography and French. Moreover I was told that if all went well I would follow these forty boys up through the school. They were already one term into their courses and doing well, so my task was to keep up the momentum.

The head, four years into his post and already with a high and well deserved reputation with the inspectorate and the education authority, laid down strict guidelines for the teaching of Maths and English and informed me that in three or four months time we would have the annual examinations in all subjects.

When the exams arrived I discovered that Mr Dawes was setting maths papers for the whole school, and that they were to be marked according to a strict and detailed code. The results for 1A were dismally poor. I could offer no excuses. The boys had been keen, had done all that I had asked of them and had presented no disciplinary problems. Their all round results were twenty per cent lower than in previous years and significantly lower than the other A-stream classes.

In a painful interview it was made clear to me that the failure was mine and mine alone. I was no longer to follow my forty boys through the school, but in the next academic year I would take on full responsibility for form 1R, the lowest stream in the school. Twenty youngsters of mixed ages all of whom would, in today's parlance, have been classified as having 'Special Needs'. Non-readers, numerically illiterate and anti-school, they were, not surprisingly, looked down on by the other boys and, on the rare occasions when they had to teach them, by other staff. To make matters worse, teaching accommodation was so tight that we were not to have our own regular classroom but were to float from room to room wherever there was an empty space. The new role was represented to me as a great opportunity to show my capabilities, but I and everyone else, both boys and staff, knew that it was a punishment for failure.

Although I had no experience or training to equip me for remedial teaching, the year that I spent with 1R turned out to be a happy and fulfilling experience. I had to fight hard for minimal equipment, but I had an immediate empathy with this neglected, miserable and, initially, anti-authority group. It may have helped that I had an understanding of their background – all but one were from coal mining families and I had a father, grandfather and uncles who had been 'down the pit' – or it may have been my obvious determination to fight the system for them, but whatever the reason we very soon became a tightly knit unit in a harsh world.

We met each morning in the main unheated cloakroom among wet macs, boots and assorted PE kit, with the fragrant smells wafting from the adjacent toilets an ever-present reminder of the lowliness of our status. We had taken over a set of lockers, one for each boy, with centrally held keys. Our first task each morning was to search out a classroom where we could work until lunchtime. Theoretically this should have been a simple matter of studying the timetable to see which of the more privileged groups were down to do woodwork, metalwork or science so leaving their own rooms vacant. In practice staff absences, school visits, dental inspections, visits from the 'nit-nurse' or the school medical officer were always liable to disrupt the timetable's smooth running and leave us roomless.

We turned the twice-daily room hunt into a game. Four boys were detailed to lurk in various parts of the school grounds, alert and watchful for signs of a vacant room. Their mission was then to report back to the cloakroom where we waited, poised with cardboard boxes stuffed full of all the necessary equipment for the day. The rules of the game were that when a place was found we had to move off quietly, even stealthily, to commandeer the unoccupied room and settle to work in the shortest possible time. Sometimes, because of an unexpected timetable change, the room's rightful owners would arrive back expecting to take back their allotted space. These occasions, rare though they were, caused considerable disruption while we argued our case before, inevitably, gathering our equipment and setting out for further migration.

The situation became farcical when we were forced to move twice in one morning, finally washing up in the assembly hall/gymnasium. Here the boys sat themselves on the floor while I resumed reading them a story. We were just getting engrossed in the latest adventure of smugglers in *Moonfleet* when thirty nubile fourth-form girls from the neighbouring girls' school, who shared some of our facilities, turned up for a PE lesson. Much to the sadness of the boys I marched them away from the delights of the hall and finished the lesson squashed in the corridor outside the headmaster's room. I vainly hoped it might focus his mind on our predicament.

With no experience in dealing with Special Needs youngsters, and no guidance from my headmaster or education authority, I pursued my own idiosyncratic course when it came to teaching. No set timetable, lessons changed without delay if interest was flagging and everything possible turned into a game. I tested the boys for basic attainments in arithmetic and reading and gave each individual a new target for improvement every month. These were recorded in a notebook each boy kept in his locker ,and while they were never made public it was soon evident that the boys were sharing their knowledge and boasting to each other about progress.

It became clear to me that progress in reading was the key to progress in all other subjects and I concentrated my efforts accordingly. We were desperately short of suitable textbooks so I collected surplus reading books from one of the local infant schools. Although of appropriate reading age, the subject matter was startlingly inappropriate! We had to produce our own reading matter. We collected a large pile of comics and the weekly storybooks that were hugely popular at the time – *Wizard*, *Rover*, *Hotspur* and the like. I used these to produce a whole series of worksheets and simplified stories. I would write these out laboriously each day while the class were playing draughts, cards or the favourite board games of Ludo or Snakes and Ladders, and then print them out on a hectograph – a primitive copying machine. This tray of gelatine combined with special ink would magically produce up to thirty copies. The class was split into five groups with the best reader in each group given responsibility for helping the others. The groups were balanced by attainment and set to compete against each other. Progress was better than I had dared to hope and it was gratifying to find boys in various quiet corners working in pairs and going over the day's worksheets.

In that second full year of my teaching career we were running an experimental eight-day timetable, one afternoon of which was designated as a clubs afternoon. On these occasions each teacher offered an activity not normally on the timetable; my contribution was chess. Nine of my group signed up to the chess club as their first choice. Encouraged by this response and having the advantage of a flexible timetable I introduced chess in the classroom as a natural follow-up to draughts on which they were already keen. We began with simple end-games – two rooks and a king against a king, king and queen against a king and so on. Only when they became adept at these did we move on to the full game. In general the boys played a rapid fire game, swapping piece for piece rather than looking a few moves ahead, but two boys developed sufficient skill to hold their own easily with the best of the A-stream boys. When, later in the year, we entered a team in the inter-school's tournament it was a 1R pupil who was the only one of our team to win all three of his games against grammar school opposition.

Our nomadic existence in the school might well have continued indefinitely had it not been for an unexpected diversion a few days after the beginning of the third term, an unannounced visit from one of our local HMIs. He came specially to see me in order to assess for himself this curious character who had made such a mess of his first two terms in such an excellent school. He was waiting for me when I arrived one morning, hot and bothered after my usual ten-mile cycle ride from home to school. After a brief introduction by the headmaster, the intimidating man came with me to meet the class. He was, no doubt, surprised to see us assembling as usual for morning registration and collection of dinner monies in a cloakroom. It was pouring with rain and as I shed my oilskins and the boys their macs I introduced the class as best I could. We did warming up exercises on the spot while we waited to see which room we were to occupy for the morning. And then the awful truth emerged – this was the morning when all the other forms were to be in their own rooms to start the maths exams. The only place the deputy head could find for us was again the gymnasium. No desks, no chairs, and no blackboard; nothing other than that which we would carry in our well travelled cardboard boxes.

I got each boy to put out his work and record cards for inspection at the back of the gym while we did our best to use the morning profitably. The boys sat on gym benches for mental arithmetic, then we split into four groups for reading lessons. One of the groups asked the inspector for help which he readily gave and when attention flagged we broke off for some impromptu drama. I recited the wonderfully evocative poem 'The Listeners' by Walter de la Mare and the boys played parts: the traveller crying out his unanswered greetings, the phantom listeners spread out on the wall bars, a disorderly group of horses clip-clopping away through the forest. The boys were quite unperturbed by the visitors' presence and responded enthusiastically to his questions. When I asked them what they would like to do next they replied with one voice, "Games!" We emptied the games box and they were soon engrossed in a variety of board games. Then the rain stopped so we collected our store of crude home-made surveying equipment and went outside to do some practical mathematics.

Apart from a short session with the headmaster the inspector stayed with us all day. We finished the afternoon with a further instalment of our *Moonfleet* serial adventure story, and so back to our cloakroom with our assortment of boxes. I spent half an hour explaining the backgrounds of the boys and discussing the progress they had made before he left me to spend further time with the head. I don't know exactly what was said but it was no doubt pretty caustic because within a matter of days we were moved into our own room.

This miracle was achieved by redesignating the medical block, a small suite of rooms with a waiting area, toilet and washing facilities, cloakroom and a room where the visiting medical officer and community nurse would carry out their infrequent inspections. The suite was fitted out with desks, cupboards, shelves and a blackboard and we moved in with due pomp and ceremony. It should have been ideal – it was permanent, well equipped, warm and self-contained – but the boys disliked it almost from the first. As the school nomads, the boys had grown to regard themselves as special, 1R against the world. Now they had lost their outcast status and with it their zest and enthusiasm. We did our best with the room, putting up pinboards, pictures and original artwork. I still enjoyed working with them, we got out of the classroom as often as we could with a variety of expeditions into the countryside, but we did not again achieve the 'fine careless rapture' of our first two terms.

I was told that the inspector had been very impressed with the progress that the boys had made, if not with the working conditions, and towards the end of term I was informed that I was to be reinstated into the A-stream. Since this was clearly intended to be a reward for good work I didn't protest – it would have been pointless anyway – and my remaining time at Alfreton was spent following the brightest boys up through the school. The only contact I had with 1R boys was when they came in decreasing numbers to the chess club.

While I welcomed the challenges of teaching in the A-stream, after a few years the teaching felt stereotyped and unadventurous and I was aware of increasing boredom. My secondary modern teaching had become routine. I was in a well-disciplined school with a head who was charismatic but gave his staff little scope for curriculum initiative. With two small daughters and a mortgage, money was tight and promotion prospects locally were limited.

It was Joyce who saw the advertisement: extra money, extra responsibility and the opportunity to work with deprived youngsters in a delightful residential setting. I had a sudden vision of such youngsters blossoming under the spell of my magnificent teaching skills and skilled casework. What is more, this wonderful work was to be in a school which had direct links with John Wesley, the founder of Methodism, so for me, as a lifelong Methodist, the job seemed tailor made. Of course, the hours would be longer. It was clear from the advertisement that as the post was for a teacher/deputy housemaster there would be a minimum of eighteen hours extraneous duties a week at evenings and weekends.

"What's new?", said Joyce. "You already spend three evenings a week teaching evening classes and doing voluntary work with the school youth club."

"But what about holidays?"

"You mean the last holiday when we took thirty boys to Ireland, or the one before that when we took fifteen boys to the Open Country Pursuits Centre? It won't be that much different and at least you'll be getting paid for all the extra hours."

So the application went in.

To my surprise not only was I not called for an interview but my referees were not even contacted. I should, of course, have left it there but somehow my interest had been aroused and I wrote a polite letter to Mr Adams, the principal, asking what further experience or qualification I might need to gain a post in his or some similar establishment. By one of those coincidences more common than we often realise, Mr Adams was shortly to attend a conference at Swanwick Hayes Conference Centre. Since our home was in Swanwick he wondered whether I might meet him. Our property was literally next to the conference centre grounds, so it could not have been more convenient, and a meeting was arranged.

Even at this distance I can clearly recall my first meeting with Dick Adams, in one of the imposing rooms in the conference centre. He stood to greet me with a firm handshake and though he was half a head shorter than my six feet two I was immediately aware of a formidable personality behind piercingly blue-grey eyes. He emphasised at once that this was not to be in any sense a formal interview but simply a chat between colleagues in the educational field. Colleagues? I was a straightforward secondary modern teacher on scale one; he was already a power in the land and an expert in his field as principal of one of two leading establishments for classifying and treating delinquent youth. What did I know about work in his field?

In the next thirty minutes or so my appalling ignorance of delinquency, Approved School Orders, classification, psychiatric treatment, social backgrounds, or indeed anything to do with the field which I had been presumptuous enough to want to join, was miserably laid bare. Having exposed my lack of knowledge my tormentor then encouraged me to talk about my present job, my interests, my family, my hopes and my ambitions. Finally came the obvious question. "Why do you want to work in an approved school?"

My self-esteem already in shreds, I could give no adequate answer. I babbled on about new challenges, a wish to help the less fortunate, new opportunities for the family away from a small village, but it didn't sound convincing even to me, and I finally trailed off into miserable silence. Summoning up a modicum of self-respect, I stood up. "I'm clearly wasting your time, I'll go—"

"Sit down!" A peremptory order. "We haven't finished. Let me enlighten you as to what the work in an approved school is like. At least you may then feel better about your present job."

He proceeded to flesh out a job description calculated to deter even the most dedicated applicant. Long hours, poor classroom conditions, anti-authority youngsters, outdated and bureaucratic Approved School Rules, shorter staff holidays, and public misunderstanding and prejudice were just the tip of the iceberg. Paradoxically, the more it appeared he was trying to put me off, the more interested I became.

"Surely there must be pluses you haven't mentioned or no-one would go into the work?"

"Well yes, of course." And as he went over some of them his enthusiasm for the work he was doing became clear. Approved schools were expanding, new establishments were being opened, the old idea of reformatories where the sole object of putting youngsters away was to punish them for their misdeeds was being swept away, and new initiatives based on a system of rewards and privileges were being developed.

"And of course," he said, "though it probably wouldn't interest you, we are heirs at Kingswood to a great tradition. The training school was originally set up in 1864 in the very building that John Wesley built as a school for the sons of his travelling preachers. The old building has been replaced, but we still use his school for the sons of Kingswood miners as a workshop."

Not interest me? As a lifelong Methodist I had a sudden rosy vision of treading the same ground as our illustrious founder. It was only later that I realised the obvious – of course Dick Adams knew of my Methodist background. He had not only dug out my original application but had contacted my referees. In those days confidential referees were just that and it was only much later that I discovered the facts.

The interview, which it clearly became, ground on. In the end I went home feeling like a wrung out dish cloth, but with an invitation to visit the school to judge for myself. And so, in due course, it was arranged that I would spend the coming Whitsuntide holiday not digging my garden as I had planned, but doing a week's voluntary, unpaid work at Kingswood. This week, purely coincidentally of course, coincided with one of the four home leaves a year which the boys then enjoyed. Instead of being faced with a hundred and twenty boys there would be no more than twenty, with cover provided by a few of the teaching staff. I was assured that the disadvantage of not seeing the whole school would be more than offset by the chance I would have to get to know a few boys to a much greater depth and to assess the atmosphere of the school in more relaxed circumstances.

My first sight of the school was far from encouraging. A huge building in Bath stone built on three sides of a square, it looked very much like some of the army barrack squares I had known in my service days. The barracks impression was heightened by a massive stone wall and the huge double gates at the entrance. I had arrived by train and local bus – not for me the luxury of a taxi from the station – and had some misgivings when none of the locals seemed to know what I was talking about when I asked for directions to Kingswood Training School. Eventually the light dawned, "Oh, you mean the reformatory – that's just down the street." What was I letting myself in for? Reformatory? A barrack square?

On the plus side, a pleasant garden on one side of the school, an avenue of mature chestnut trees that I learned later dated back to John Wesley, and a spacious playing field in the distance softened the overall impression. While I was standing absorbing the atmosphere a well-spoken youngster approached me and asked, "Excuse me, Sir, are you Mr Stanway? I've been asked to wait for you and show you over the estate."

This polite, obviously intelligent and certainly well spoken young man showed me to my accommodation, a pleasant, quiet guest room in a flat next to the dormitory the boys were using. After waiting patiently while I deposited my case he proceeded to give me a guided tour, chatting freely and informatively all the time while showing me over the whole of the estate. I was impressed by the fact that he had been entrusted with keys to various rooms and by the fact that before we left my room he advised me to lock the doors, "We do have some thieves here, Sir.

It's best not to take chances." He told me, without prompting, something of his own history – truanting, persistent petty theft and finally robbery with violence. "But I know better now, Sir. I shall soon be going on licence."

Surely any establishment that could produce such changes in such a confirmed delinquent would be a wonderful place in which to work. The euphoria continued even when I saw the classroom block, a group of somewhat decrepit concrete buildings with corrugated asbestos roofs, depressing furniture, overhead gas heaters which I knew to be inefficient and damp-producing and not a single bright picture on the walls to lighten the atmosphere. By contrast the gymnasium was spacious and well equipped, and a covered area next to it led to an indoor swimming bath, which on that hot summer day was cool and inviting.

And so a delightful day rolled on. The rest of the boys returned before teatime from a trip out in the school's Austin Welfarer bus, together with two members of staff who welcomed me with open arms. Of course I was there to offer unpaid assistance and give them some time off, but I had no sense of being taken advantage of. The boys were a bit boisterous after their day out by the sea but the cooked high tea shared by boys and staff was adequate and the atmosphere pleasant and relaxed. I was left in charge during the evening, polishing up my skills at table tennis and snooker, and the teacher in charge returned at nine o'clock to usher the boys to bed. I was surprised to see that there were no night staff but it was pointed out that since my flat was next to where the boys were sleeping that counted as night cover. If there was an emergency I would be expected to cope, calling out the deputy head if necessary.

I was given some guidance on procedure by John Williams, the PE teacher, one of three male staff on duty over the holiday and by appearances the senior person in charge. He was a boisterous, cheerful, rugby-playing Welshman who was clearly totally confident in his work and very willing to share his experiences and insights with a newcomer. Impatient with bureaucracy he had no great liking for pettifogging rules, but it soon became clear that he loved his job and that he always had the best interests of the boys at heart. In several conversations he put me wise as to some of the pitfalls possible when dealing with intelligent delinquent youngsters. In particular he stressed that while I was new, inexperienced and wet behind the ears I must be careful when dealing with them on a one-to-one basis.

"We've got one or two little blighters who, given the chance, will be only too ready to make nasty allegations. Watch your back!"

"Surely not with this group here, they're a super lot."

"They are, but I'm telling you – don't take risks."

I was not so naïve that I did not know what he was talking about, but little did I know then how important his advice was to be later.

On the fourth evening of my stay I was invited for a meal with John and his delightful wife, Blodwen. It was a pleasant, relaxed evening but when John and I walked back to school it was to find a minor crisis under way – young Kevin, who had had a row with a mate over a game of snooker, had been discovered missing at suppertime. We got in John's car and did a quick tour round the estate and the local streets. When we didn't find him we called at the local police station to report him missing. The procedure was simple and clearly well known: a brief description of his dress, build, home address, date of birth and any relevant details we wished to add and we were on our way back to school.

"Have a last look round before you go to bed," said John. "I have a feeling he won't have gone far. Give me a call if he turns up."

Sure enough, when I did my last round up I found a bedraggled, wet, miserable-looking boy hiding under the stairs. I took him upstairs into my flat and put the kettle on while I rang John on the internal phone. He was over in a quarter of an hour or so and we had a coffee while he was getting Kevin's story straight. Apparently he had not even left the school grounds, and had come back into the building because he was wet and miserable. John took him downstairs, gave him a shower and put him to bed.

The next day the episode was fully written up in the logbook and the boy's file. John was meticulous in detailing the times. The fifteen minutes between my telephoning John and his appearance in my flat seemed to have been telescoped into three minutes but I didn't bother to argue about such trivial details and I was able to log the whole incident mentally as a useful learning curve.

And so passed a very pleasant six days. I accompanied the boys on trips out in the locality, organised five-a-side football matches, played numerous games of snooker and table tennis and supervised swimming periods. I saw Dick Adams a few times during the week and then, on the day before I was due to return home, he invited me to meet two of the managers. This turned out to be a formal interview but not at all formidable, and I was offered a post as teacher/deputy housemaster if I wanted it. By that time my mind was made up, but I was advised to talk it over with my wife before making a final decision.

I went home on cloud nine, helped by the fact that I was given a claim form for my travel and out of pocket expenses. Since I had slept in the school, had taken all my meals with the boys and had the various excursion expenses paid as we went, my claim was minimal. It did occur to me as I journeyed home that in six days I had put in something over a hundred hours and saved the school a small fortune in overtime — that is if overtime was recognised and paid which, as I discovered later, it wasn't!

And so the die was cast. If Joyce had any doubts she hid them very well and our two daughters were too young to be worried. I expected to start my new job in September, but unfortunately missed the deadline for giving due notice by two day. My school, and the education authority, refused to waive the rules and I had to tell Kingswood that I could not start work till the following January. I offered to withdraw my application but was told by Dick Adams that, "To get the man we want we are prepared to wait." What a charmer! I did wonder what the staff who would have to cover my absence would think but I happily confirmed my acceptance and began to prepare for my departure by reading up all I could find about juvenile delinquency, court procedures, approved school history and the notorious 1933 Approved School Rules.

CHAPTER 2

And so to Kingswood...

We arrived at Kingswood on 31 December 1954, at the same time as our furniture which had been collected two days earlier. We had our brand new Ford Popular loaded to the gunwales with oddments, our two small daughters and Joyce's mum, who was coming to give us a hand with settling in. No problems with child seats, or even seat belts in those days, but we did have difficulty getting our youngest, ten months old and very determined, back into the car after we stopped for a picnic. She clung to the roof and set up a screaming fit that was something to hear. We got her in eventually but she had her revenge by being sick over her mum's new outfit. There was no motorway in those days so it was a weary party which arrived to find that the furniture removers had left our goods and chattels wherever it was most convenient to them and certainly not in the places we had indicated on the carefully labelled boxes. At the height of the chaos the deputy head knocked at the door to welcome us, and to tell me that I was expected on duty in Byron House at seven o'clock the next morning. I had hoped for a day's grace, but in fairness the staff had been waiting six months for me to arrive!

Byron House, where I was to act as deputy housemaster, occupied most of the top floor and part of the ground floor of the central arm of the main building. The top floor had a common room, a quiet room, a staff sleeping-in room and an attached, quite spacious, flat for the housemaster, house matron and their family. The flat and the boys' quarters were separated by a landing and a wide stone staircase.

When the housemaster came out of his flat to show me the ropes things ran like clockwork. We walked the length of the dormitory and a tap on each row of beds was the signal for the boys to swing their legs from under the blankets. As we walked back, each row in order turned their mattresses and began to fold blankets in neat regulated piles. Then began a busy half hour of sweeping, dusting and cleaning before, at a given signal, the boys clattered downstairs for their morning wash and teeth cleaning. I wondered why three or four of the older boys had no morning jobs, but it was explained that they were the house captain and his helpers. Ten minutes to relax, then boys and staff trooped down the stairs to join the other two houses in the communal dining room. It seemed to me that the happy, relaxed attitude I had observed six months earlier did not apply to Byron House, but I assured myself that this was probably because the boys had only just returned from Christmas home leave.

After breakfast, eaten in what seemed to my overstretched nerves to be a sullen silence, we had half an hour of free time before morning assembly. I tried to make conversation with one of the youngsters I remembered having met six months previously. Then I had believed we had made reasonable contact, but now he shied away from my pleasantries like a frightened gazelle. Later on he did manage a few words. "Please, please don't talk to me on my own, Sir, you'll get me thumped." My spirits sank. What on earth was going on? I tried to assure him of my protection, but I could see that he had no confidence that he would be safe.

I had a reasonable day in the classroom, teaching the full day from nine to five with an hour and a half for lunch. My class of fifteen responded to my efforts with quiet resignation if not enthusiasm. I made a point of learning each boy's name during the first half hour and set them a series of simple maths and English tests as a preliminary to constructing individual worksheets – necessary because text books appeared to be non-existent. I could find no detailed records of attainment or intelligence testing, but hoped these would be available in their individual files kept in the central office. Until I had the opportunity of studying this data I had to improvise.

My teaching duties done, I went home to ponder the mysteries of the day. I was not too dismayed by the classroom situation, but had a nagging feeling that things were far from well in the house set-up. My helpful next-door neighbour, who had an enviable mastery of his mainly ESN class, was informative but not encouraging. He described Byron House, where he had undertaken occasional relief duties, as ' a mess'. A forceful house captain, backed up by a small coterie of hitmen, was in effective control. Providing staff were prepared to give him his head, turn a blind eye to the rackets he was running and allow him and his cronies a few special privileges, the organisation would run smoothly and staff would have an easy time. Robert, my neighbour, made it clear that after several failed attempts to change things he had reluctantly fallen in with the system. "Of course it would be different if I was permanently attached to the house," he admitted, "but that will be your job. For what it's worth take it steady and, for God's sake, watch your back!"

I spent a restless night pondering how I was to tackle the next morning's duty on my own. Surely I had enough on my plate without stirring up a hornet's nest right at the start. In any case I was only the deputy housemaster, and still wet behind the ears at that. Did I have the right to follow any other course? Then I remembered little Gary's terror when I had tried to speak to him. Surely it couldn't be right that he should be so obviously bullied? In the event I settled for a fatal compromise that satisfied neither me nor the house captain, Phillip. I told him I would go along with the system for the time being but that I wasn't happy with it. I intended changes in the future when I was on duty.

The morning went reasonably enough, but I had a sick feeling inside that I had failed the test. This half-hearted fudge convinced no one, and I could tell from the gleam in Phillip's eyes that he had scented an easy victory. I tried talking reasonably to him in the half hour after breakfast, but it was clear from his barely concealed sneer that I was wasting my breath. It wasn't what he said, for that couldn't have been more co-operative.

"Yes, Sir, of course, Sir, I quite understand, Sir, but it would be much easier for you, Sir, if we worked together... After all, I am the house captain..."

Battle lines were being drawn. The next day was the disastrous Wednesday previously described. I was sure that Phillip was the driving force behind my humiliation but I couldn't pin him down. He might have been sitting next to the brick-throwing boy, but he remained a model of apparent decorum. He did, however, twist the knife at dinnertime. "I'm sorry you had such a bad morning, Sir. Would you like me to have a word with the trouble makers?"

"No, Phillip, that's my job, not yours."

"Very good, Sir, but please remember that I offered to help."

Worse was to follow during that awful week. I staggered through to Friday when I was on dinner duty for the whole school, supervising all three houses in the dining room. I have no doubt that my apprehension showed, but the first course passed by fairly peacefully. Then trouble began to erupt in various, unconnected parts of the room. A plate clattered to the floor; a chair was mysteriously knocked over; a minor fight broke out at the far side. As I moved over to deal with this last disturbance a small shower of plum stones hit the back of my neck. At that moment the headmaster of the training school, Dick Adams' deputy, entered the room and order descended like magic. He made no comment on my miserable efforts at control, but stayed chatting amiably until that horrendous dinner was finally at an end. Phillip, of course, rubbed salt into my wounds by coming up to sweep up the stones with a brush and dustpan.

As I was not on weekend duty, my miserable working week ended there. Two days to recuperate before the whole cycle began again. I tried to hide my humiliation and dismay from Joyce without any success – the wounds had gone too deep. She expressed a confidence in my ability to succeed that lifted my spirits somewhat.

By Tuesday, when I was next to be on house duty, my fears had returned in full force. This time Phillip's tactics were different. He initiated a deliberate 'go slow' tactic during the morning cleaning. Every job took twice as long as usual to finish. We were late for breakfast, late for the regular school parade on the square, and late to morning assembly. Not a word was spoken by the deputy head who was conducting the assembly, but I was all too aware of the looks going around the boys and staff. My calamities of the first few days were already part of school folklore, and though staff were sympathetic and generally helpful they too must have been wondering when the next calamity was going to happen. Phillip, naturally, was as helpful as ever. "Sorry we're late, Sir. We just couldn't seem to get going this morning, we'll do better tomorrow."

Of course they would. Stanway wouldn't be on house duty – back to the old tried and tested system.

Another two days and I was again on morning duty. This time the ruling clique decided on a surprising new tactic: sweet co-operation. It's true there was a degree of sullen resentment from a few boys who had hoped for better things from me, but cleaning, washing, breakfast and morning parade went like clockwork and Byron House was the first ready for morning inspection and assembly. "I'm glad you allowed me to help this morning," said Phillip, "I hope you're pleased?"

"Well no, I'm not," I thought, but said nothing aloud. The stark reality was now becoming clear. I could work with the system, which at least gave stability and order, or I could work to change it.

If I was going to take this latter course, how should I go about it? I would get little help from the housemaster, who was clearly resigned to accepting the status quo, and did not feel I could get any assistance from Dick Adams. I certainly was not going to confess to him after a fortnight that the job was beyond my capabilities. Nor could I share with him my worries and concerns about a system which seemed to condone, if not actively encourage, bullying. I had no doubt that the principal knew exactly what was going on in the training school. It is true that he had delegated day-to-day accountability for the school to the headmaster, but he was still in overall charge and though his visits were infrequent he had an uncanny knack of being on the spot at the most relevant times. In my first fortnight he had 'just happened' to have to walk through Byron House to the Bursar's office on the morning that all had been sweetness and light.

"Very peaceful this morning. Phillip seems to be co-operating." Oh bitter, bitter shame; he knows of my humiliations. "Do you like the present system?"

"No, no, no!", I wanted to shout. But I said no such thing; indeed I mumbled something about wanting to find my feet before suggesting any changes.

"Ah well, we'll see how things go then. I'll be very interested to see how you progress over the next six months."

Six months! With the present ragged state of my nerves I would be hard pressed to survive for six weeks!

If the schoolroom work had pursued the same dangerous course as the house duties, I do not believe I would have survived, but my regular class group of twenty-two proved much easier to deal with. I found, hidden away, a reasonable set of English textbooks. For mathematics I reproduced the sets of arithmetic worksheets which had first been worked by 1R in Alfreton, and started these lads off on individual programmes. Since the exercises were designed to give success by having starting points within the boys' capabilities, they went down well.

Timetabling for the schoolroom work was essentially simple. We had three full-time teachers and three regular classroom groups, split broadly according to intelligence and attainment. In addition we had a relief teacher who would step in to cover teachers or instructors on holiday, a few part-time language teachers who took groups of three or four students to study French and German, and the deputy head who took on a half-time teaching commitment. The flexible timetable allowed some interchanges between classes for various specialist subjects. I, for instance, taught French to class one and Geography to class three. While I was teaching these sessions my own class would be in science lessons in the laboratory or music in the assembly hall, equipped as it was with a reasonable piano. Wednesday was changeover day, when all the over-fifteens came back into the classroom for their compulsory, but much disliked, academic work and the under-fifteens were split between the four trade training departments.

After my first disastrous Wednesday I prepared for the next as if for a siege. Work laid out on the tables, pens and paper at the ready. The atmosphere was strained, with regular incidents of minor revolt, and by the end of the day my nerve ends were quivering, but there was no repeat of the first disaster. Curiously to me the most relaxed lesson was the class reading done as a group exercise. I had brought with me from my previous school a large box of various textbook samples suitable for different requirements. A set of the adventure story *Moonfleet*, read aloud to the class, caught the imagination and soon became a regular standby when boredom or discontent was setting in. Picking only the competent readers or reading aloud myself I always ensured that we finished at an exciting point to keep the interest alive.

Another useful standby when the going got tough was the flexibility of the curriculum, which gave teachers the freedom to introduce whatever they wanted. All teachers of a few years experience develop a repertoire of 'one off' lessons that have gone down well in the past and can be trotted out in an emergency. Teachers of my generation had especial need of such lessons as we very seldom had the luxury of supply teachers when colleagues were absent. Only long absences were ever 'covered' and short absences were dealt with in a variety of ways. Classes could be divided up and re-allocated wherever there was room, but the first casualty was the precious 'marking and preparation' lessons. Thus, at the drop of a hat, you could find yourself dealing with a different class in a different room with an unfamiliar subject. In the absence of guidance from the usual teacher it was usually appropriate to fall back on a previously prepared topic, sometimes related to the timetabled subject but more often to a particular hobby horse of your own. It was this experience that now stood me in good stead, so that from time to time the reluctant academics would be treated to a lesson on the possibilities of space travel, the solar system, Boadicea, the Gallic wars or even the latest episode of *Dick Barton – Special Agent*!

So the days ground on in that first miserable month. While my regular classroom work began to take off the department boys always resented being removed from the work they really enjoyed. They were, in any case, marshalled by Phillip and his henchmen to be awkward. Even so, careful preparation, lavish use of the hectograph for prepared lessons at all stages, and a readiness to fall back on some interesting diversions avoided the disasters of my first Wednesday. All in all, my hours in the classroom became more and more fulfilling and even more important I began to make some genuine relationships with the four Byron House boys who were in class two. They were by no means able to escape the domination of the 'gang' but the signs of revolt were beginning.

As my battered ego began to recover we started on some practical surveying work around the Kingswood estate, hopefully to be linked at some stage to a technical drawing course. The woodwork instructor, who was by coincidence not only a Methodist but a fellow local preacher, helped me produce a set of surveying instruments far superior to the primitive efforts I had cobbled together with 1R. Theodolites, clinometer, ranging rods and plane tables with which we were able to survey the grounds, work out the heights of buildings and the gradients of the estate roads. It seemed to genuinely interest the boys and led on naturally to simple geometry and trigonometry by which we were able to check the results of the scale drawings. This was something quite new and strange to almost all of them and to my surprise, they lapped it up! No doubt they caught something of my own enthusiasm but equally important was the fact that although they were woefully retarded in basic skills they had the intelligence to cope well with the more abstract ideas.

Unfortunately, our surveying work finished precipitously when half a dozen boys took the opportunity to disappear into the bushes for a cigarette and were discovered by the headmaster.

What progress there was in the classroom was offset by continuing chaos in the house. What was worse was the growing conviction that I had made a catastrophic mistake in leaving what was, in retrospect, an attractive lifestyle: a well disciplined school, attractive new home, delightful surroundings, friendly colleagues, good neighbours, and family close at hand to give support. If it had not been for the steadfast and unwavering support of Joyce I could not have gone on. Whatever her own reservations and worries she stoutly maintained that we would work things out and that what I was attempting in Byron House was the right approach.

When I was off duty Joyce did her best to make sure I could rest and recuperate. It was in the first fortnight in a brief hour when I was resting after a stormy morning before returning to the fray that there was a knock at our door, and a stranger, to Joyce, asked if he could see Mr Stanway.

"If it's important, yes. Otherwise, no, he's having a much needed break before afternoon school."

"Oh, that's all right. I'll see him some other time."

"Who shall I say called?"

"Mr Adams, and may I say how pleased I am to see you and welcome you to Kingswood."

I believe Dick Adams at that moment marked Joyce out as a determined and forceful character. He was certainly neither hurt nor insulted by her attitude, being a man who had no liking or respect for boot-lickers.

Hard on the heels of Joyce's first encounter with Dick Adams, I had what could have been the nail in the coffin of my career at Kingswood. It was a bitterly cold January morning. I opened the classroom door, turned on the overhead gas heater – an operation never performed until we were safely installed in the classroom – and started the usual series of exercises on the spot until the place warmed up. Work started after a few minutes and I was busy at my desk marking a boy's work when there was a peremptory knocking on the table at the back of the room. I looked up to see a tall, military looking gentleman glaring at me. I had met his type many times before in my army career. The orderly officer doing his rounds. What was such a character doing in my classroom? I was soon left in no doubt. Without so much as a by your leave he rapped out a military style order – "Instructor, you need fresh air. Open some of these windows."

I had already been subjected to two hours of house duty with Phillip and his conspirators at their most difficult. I was in no mood for this. Tolerance snapped.

"I have no idea who you are but this is my classroom and what we need at the moment is not fresh air but some warmth! I'll open some windows when I'm ready."

"For your information I'm Brigadier Johnson, your visiting manager for the month. I'll leave you to it – for now!"

Whoops! What other bricks could I drop in that first month? Curiously, although I didn't know it at the time, my encounter with the Brigadier did me no harm at all in the long run. In fact, quite the opposite. Many months later it came to my ears that the Brigadier's succinct summing up of me to the chairman of the managers was, "That man, Stanway, is officer material!"

Obviously the good Brigadier could not have been aware of the details of my own army career – perhaps I had glossed over it in my curriculum vitae…

. . . . .

When I was called up for compulsory military service in 1942 I was among the first recruits to be assessed by a number of psychological and intelligence tests in order to determine the most suitable for rapid promotion to officer training. By good fortune, or perhaps because they got the papers mixed up, I was one of just two from the seven hundred or so intake at the Norwich barracks who were selected to see the Colonel in charge. No doubt he wished to check out the efficiency of the new selection system as compared to the rubric that had served the forces so well in the past – public school, previous background, accent, and those indefinable qualities of leadership beloved of generations of appointment boards. And so, in double quick time, two somewhat bewildered recruits were summoned to appear before the Company Commander and the Colonel himself.

By a most curious coincidence, my friend Pete and I could well have passed for twins. Both six feet two, as thin as beanpoles and both wearing army-issue steel-rimmed spectacles to correct extreme short sight. In addition our uniforms, regulation battle-dress, were ludicrously ill fitting. The only guide the Quartermaster Sergeant had used in fitting us out was our height so that, though the sleeves and trouser legs were long enough, those were the only correct measurements in the whole ensemble. There was enough spare material to make a second uniform for each of us. The jackets' necklines hung like horse collars, the trouser waists would have accommodated two army-issue pillows and the trouser legs hung over and completely concealed our regulation gaiters. At least they also hid the fact that neither of us had come near to achieving the 'spit and polish' boots so beloved of old sweats. To complete the sorry picture there was a practice alert for German parachutists in operation so we had to parade in full kit with respirators at the ready.

The Regimental Sergeant Major who was to march us in blanched in horror at the sight of these supposed elite recruits who would, if all went well with their training, be the leaders of the new order. He made a few ineffectual adjustments to our dress and ordered us in: "Left right, left right—halt, left turn—stand at ease." Our uniforms were already at ease, but we endeavoured to relax a little and to look at least reasonably intelligent.

The two officers peered in astonishment at the ludicrous apparitions in front of them and then, in obvious disbelief, re-read the test results showing our top grade intelligence. Finally, after what seemed an age, "Sergeant Major!"

"Sir."

"Have we got the right men?"

"That's what the papers say, Sir."

"My God—!"

I can only imagine that the Colonel expressed such reservations that our entry into officer training was delayed. I was sent on to Lincoln to do a fourteen-week infantry signals course with the Sherwood Foresters while Pete went back to his native Essex. Nevertheless, in due course, I completed a pre-Officer Cadet Training Unit course at Wrotham in Kent and was posted to Catterick to begin the long and very interesting course which would lead to the exalted rank of Second Lieutenant and so on to glory. All went well until the obligatory battle camp in the Lake District, where we had to show our leadership qualities under battle conditions. Physically demanding certainly, but I could cope with that. However, when it was my turn to lead my platoon into 'battle' I was a disastrous failure. As we set off in blinding rain across muddy fells the sergeant overseeing our section yelled "Gas!" and we immediately had to put on our respirators. In the driving rain my army specs and the respirator goggles were so misted over that I could barely see five yards in front of me. We blundered along what I fondly imagined to be the best route to the enemy we were attacking, only to find that I had led my men through a well-marked minefield which, together with a well positioned enemy machine gun post I had failed to notice, resulted in the complete annihilation of my troop.

Officer material indeed!

. . . . .

This was my first encounter with any of the managers since my initial interview. I was to get to know some of them very well in the future. Without exception they were helpful and interested in the welfare of the school. This was only to be expected since they were voluntary and unpaid and the job earned more brickbats than bouquets. One challenge they all faced was to grasp the sordid reality of the backgrounds of the boys, far removed from their own middle- or upper-class lives. Apart from the Brigadier we had a Colonel, an eminent psychiatrist, a retired senior executive of Indian Railways, a titled lady, a barrister and half a dozen well-heeled businessmen. Their position at Kingswood was a curious one. Theoretically they had absolute control of all the boys sent to the school. As soon as a youngster was made the subject of an Approved School Order the parents lost their control and responsibility for care, treatment, food, clothes and the whole mechanism of living were handed over first to the classifying school and later to whichever school the boy was allocated. Although the managers had responsibility on paper, in practice they handed this over to the headmaster. He had to keep a daily logbook, which was open to the inspection of the managers at any time, and detailed reports were presented at a monthly meeting.

Three of the managers became much more closely involved in the running of the school when it was decided that they would be invited to attend monthly house meetings to discuss boys' grades. As an indication of the boys' progress they were expected to pass through three grades known accurately, if not imaginatively, as one, two and three. The general idea was that each boy should move from grade three, where all the boys started when they came to the school, to grade one, at which point they would be ready to be licensed. Progress was reviewed regularly, but in detail at a monthly meeting in each house. At these, reports from everyone who had dealings with the boy were considered and contributions invited from the boy. The headmaster or deputy would chair the meeting and sum up. And so the boy's grade for the next month was decided.

This system had a good deal of merit in that it gave each boy something to aim at and was some indication of progress. It did, however, have its weaknesses. This was brought home to me at my first full group meeting in Byron House. Phillip and his three principal cronies were warmly congratulated for their efforts in the departments, their co-operation in the house and their degree of responsibility towards younger boys. Not one boy in the house took the opportunity to mention the bullying and rackets conducted by or on behalf of Phillip. It was then that I realised the scale of the problem I was facing and the weakness of the weapons at my disposal. Phillip enjoyed the hard, physical work of the stonemasonry department and was proud of his handicraft. In the classroom in my Wednesday group he sailed through the work that I set him with ease. His results were good and his work immaculate. So when asked to comment on his classroom performance I was in a genuine dilemma. The house-master had already given him high praise for his co-operation and helpfulness. His building prowess earned praise. But what of his victims? They were sitting in sullen silence with one brave soul shutting his eyes and putting his hands over his ears when the glowing report was being read – gestures redolent of utter disbelief. I tried to draw the youngster into the discussion by a direct approach.

"David, I think you have something you want to say. Would you like to speak up?"

The only response was an immediate denial, but watching the look that passed between Phillip and his main henchmen I realised all too well that my blundering approach had hindered rather than helped. Later that evening, with Phillip safely out of earshot, David came rather fearfully to me and begged me never again to single him out in a meeting. We had a furtive discussion with David glancing around from time to time to check whether we were being observed. "You don't know what it's like, Sir, when you're not about."

I couldn't imagine it being any worse than when I was about, but I could see that I was going to get nowhere at that point and so withdrew to consider my options. They seemed pretty bleak. It was clear that Phillip and his cronies were indeed ruling the roost and I suspected that they were also running a number of protection rackets. But there was no proof. Faced with a wall of silence it was proving difficult to gather any.

As I got to know the housemaster better he admitted privately that he was not happy with the present system, which he knew had gone too far but was one he had initially condoned as a way of enlisting co-operation. I could understand and even sympathise with his difficulties. Six months with no regular deputy and all the extra duties that entailed, coupled with a succession of particularly difficult youngsters, had worn him down. They would have tried the patience of a saint! I could well see that the order imposed by his formidable house captain and his henchmen at least gave him some breathing space. He was, in any case, looking for less stressful work in the social work field and had applied to be superintendent of a small children's home in a remand centre.

His wife, the house matron, was fiercely protective of her husband and very much against taking any steps that might upset the calm atmosphere of the house. This, she was quick to point out, was the general rule when anyone other than myself was on duty. With their new post in mind they needed their present good references and were not prepared to put those at risk. They both knew that the mistakes they had made with Phillip were not acceptable; they were deeply unhappy about them and would not repeat them in their next post. It seemed I would have to bide my time before much needed changes could be put into use.

The Easter Bank Holiday of 1956 should have been a joyous occasion, for we had a week's holiday planned when we had anticipated returning to Derbyshire with happy tales of our first few months and of expanding horizons to come. Instead I could see nothing but disasters and defeat ahead. Joyce, of course, was made of sterner stuff and convinced that we could win through together. In the meantime we put on the best possible face to friends and family. "Of course we are having a few problems," said Joyce, "only to be expected but it's going great."

If only—

My first day's duty after the holiday was the worst I had experienced so far. It started with the usual chaos of an organised 'go slow'. I was desperately trying to cope and comprehensively failing when Dick Adams, with his usual immaculate timing, appeared in the dormitory and, polite as ever, asked if I minded if he stayed. Yes I did, I had no wish for him to witness my humiliation, but I could hardly say so and he tucked himself into an unobtrusive corner while the battle raged. Ten minutes later, for no observable reason, there was a sudden outbreak of peace and calm and the proper routine of the day slipped into place.

"What happened to bring this about?", asked Dick Adams.

I had a fleeting idea that I might claim some magic touch but rejected it as being an insult to intelligence. Just as well I did for at this point, appearing out of nowhere, came Phillip, full of obsequious apologies.

"Sorry, Sir, I wasn't paying proper attention to my house captain responsibilities. It'll be all right now, Sir."

Of course it would. Phillip was now in control.

It was at that moment that I realised that I could not go on at Kingswood without drastic changes to the regime in Byron House. How were these to be achieved? While a peaceful breakfast proceeded, Dick Adams questioned me gently about my attitudes and impressions. I maintained my equanimity until he said, "You do seem to have more problems than other staff in the house, Eric. Why do you think that is?"

A sudden rage boiled up. Did he not know? Did he not care? Was this not his school? If I had stopped to think I would have realised that this was quite unfair. Of course he was the principal of two schools, but the training school was long established with a proud history and an independent board of management. Day-to-day running had been delegated to a headmaster and his staff. It was true that one of the school's three houses had effectively been taken over by a group of determined adolescents, but the other two houses were running effectively and successfully. Clumsy, heavy-handed interference could easily have upset the whole apple cart.

All these considerations occurred later. On that fateful morning all the frustrations of the past few months boiled up

. "You simply do not understand, *sir*, what it is like to work in a situation where a sixteen-year-old house captain and his cronies are in control."

I raged on for some minutes and then realised that I had been provoked into indiscretions I had not intended. I subsided into uneasy silence and desperately tried to backtrack. "Perhaps I should go along with the system," I mumbled.

"Is that what you want?"

"No it isn't, but I can't stand things the way they are. It's coming to the point where I must move on while I still have a modicum of self-respect."

"I hope not. When you were appointed I had great hopes of you." Great hopes indeed!

"Well, I'm sorry to disappoint you."

"Did I say I was disappointed? You've only been here five minutes."

He tried further words of encouragement, quite astonishing to my ears. Telling me, for instance, of difficulties he had had when starting as a junior member of staff. It was all to no avail. I had the sick feeling that I had been pushed into saying far too much, that as the youngest and most junior member of staff I had let down my colleagues and, in particular, the housemaster who, although he had lost effective control of his house, was a caring, compassionate man who, in different circumstances, would have so much to offer.

I went home in misery and confusion, and gave Joyce the whole sad story. She was all for tackling Dick Adams straight away to see what he had in mind. I dissuaded her from this course, but from that point began a surreptitious scanning of the *Times Educational Supplement* for a way out from my impossible situation. For the first time in all our married life I did not take Joyce fully into my confidence. I could, in all truth, see no way forward. We could go back to Derbyshire – I would even be welcome at my old school – but we had no house, no reserves of money and it would all be too humiliating after we had left with such high hopes.

There was no comfort to be found in our local church, where I felt we were regarded as interlopers. We had no close friends on the staff and nowhere to turn for comfort. I quit the marital bed and spent night after night on the sitting room sofa. Joyce would come down to make a cup of tea and I would reject her advances and send her to bed in tears.

It was at that lowest point that I came across a job made in heaven. It was in Basildon new town, in Essex. A job with a new house attached for a teacher/youth leader, half time in each post, it seemed tailor made and I promptly sent off for details. They were all I had hoped for. The teaching responsibilities were in a new comprehensive school, the youth work was in a splendidly equipped new building and, all in all, it seemed ideal. With high hopes but, at the same time, a heavy heart, I filled in the application form, with a note to Dick Adams, for I had to use him as a referee, but not a word to Joyce. After all, I reasoned, if nothing came of it she need never know and if I got the job it would be a splendid surprise. What idiotic tomfoolery and cowardice on my part. I could not keep it up. I lasted a week and then confessed all.

Joyce was furious but loving, furious because I had not discussed things with her, but loving because she could see and understand the depths of my despair. This time no words of mine could stop her from going to Dick Adams. She stormed up to his bungalow and spent two hours in discussion. I never knew quite what was said but she came back with the light of battle still in her eyes. When I pressed her to tell me what had happened she simply said, "Wait and see, but one way or another it will be all right in the end."

In quite a short time I was called for interview at County Hall, Chelmsford, and invited to bring my wife to look at a possible house. This time there were to be no secrets. Interviews were to be held over two days, so an urgent message was sent to Joyce's mum to come down to look after the children. Joyce and I set off for Essex.

I was quite encouraged when, in conversation with the district youth organiser, he informed me that he too was a Methodist lay preacher. I thought I would be home and dry as I had good teaching experience and had run a successful voluntary youth club in Derbyshire, but not only was I not offered the post, I did not even make it to the second day. The two men and one woman who were weeding out the applicants from the long list to leave just three for the main panel asked a series of such pertinent questions about my work at Kingswood that they clearly had a full knowledge of my disciplinary catastrophes in Byron House. This was confirmed later by my fellow Methodist, who told me that the reference from my principal was, to say the least, lukewarm.

Back to Kingswood, for my part in deep depression but for Joyce with no regrets, just a renewed determination to make a go of things. "Just you wait, things are going to improve. Go and talk things over with Dick Adams."

So I did.

I tackled him first about his confidential reference. To my complete surprise he had it beside him and pushed it across to me to read. Common practice now but unheard of then. What he wrote would certainly have put off any panel looking for someone who could keep control of rumbustious youngsters but I could not fault its accuracy. The last paragraph, however, ran along the lines that, although my career at Kingswood so far was a failure, he believed I would in due time be a great asset to the school. He also told me that I had a wife in a thousand and that I should go back and treasure her!

To my further surprise he went on to ask what I would do in the training school if I was given a free hand. Since I had considered youth work in Essex, what about starting a youth club in the school? If I would consider it I would be taken off Byron House and given full scope to run the new venture. I was astonished and agreed at once to go away and formulate plans for such a venture, a unique development in the Approved School Service. I went down the hill from the Adams bungalow with light steps and a sudden burst of enthusiasm to give Joyce the good news.

"Well there you are, I thought something like this might happen."

What had she talked to Dick Adams about?

One immediate and pleasurable result of the sudden lightening of the atmosphere was that I was restored to marital harmony and the marital bed. I had not of course been banished from it by Joyce – it was my own reaction to the black despair, which had overtaken me – but I was welcomed back and once again slept in peace and love with my guardian angel. Kate noticed. "Why is daddy not sleeping downstairs now. Is he not feeling poorly any more?"

"Well he's certainly feeling better," said Joyce with exquisite tact. And I was. Curiously, even the frosty atmosphere in the church began to thaw. Could it be that the fault had been ours and that people were now simply responding to our more relaxed attitude?

Although I was full of enthusiasm for the prospects opening up before me, it was going to be a few weeks before arrangements could be formulated and approved and the necessary minimum equipment got together, and before that there was still

Byron House. Somehow, now that there was an end in sight, the prospect of daily duties, with all the attendant humiliations, did not seem so formidable. In any case there were slight but very definite signs that there was a significant section of the house who were no longer willing to tolerate Phillip and his henchmen.

One of the leaders of this mini revolt was Gary, whom I had met on my first visit and who had been so afraid of my speaking to him. He had begun by refusing to make his contribution to the house funds, which everyone knew was really a private account for Phillip and his henchmen. He had received a considerable 'going over' behind the bike shed but it made no difference and when he was again threatened, three of his mates came to his defence. Only a small hole in the dyke, but Phillip's authority was definitely beginning to slip. He must have held a council of war because he began to devise new ways of causing disruption.

Whether it was common in other approved schools I know not, but in Kingswood it was standard practice at suppertime to have evening prayers in the house common rooms. Not usually a problem, but on my very first evening duty after my heart-to-heart with Adams we were, as usual, murmuring the Lord's Prayer together when there was a sudden silence after the word 'art'. "Our Father which art—" and I was left to complete the prayer on my own apart from two brave souls who had either misunderstood their instructions or were not disposed to obey. I let it pass without comment. The next night there was clearly supposed to be a concerted stop after 'bread', but this was a step too far for a fair number of boys who had Sunday School or church experience and were not prepared to go along with the instructions. Perhaps they had had enough of being bossed about or perhaps they were simply sorry for me, but whatever their motivation it was another crack in the control system.

Another pinprick against Stanway misfired spectacularly. It was again suppertime. The cups of cocoa and Bath buns were being peacefully consumed and I was circulating fairly happily among the tables when I paused briefly for a word with Phillip and his coterie. I was about to offer a pleasant greeting when Phillip, apparently chatting amicably to his cronies, said in quite a carrying voice, certainly intended for me to hear, "Did you know Stanners' wife's a fucking prostitute?"

Too stupid to be taken seriously but I lost my temper, and almost control. I hoisted him bodily out of his chair and put him against the wall but off the floor.

"Now say that again—"

"Sorry Sir, sorry, I didn't mean it. Don't hit me!"

I didn't, which was fortunate. Had I punched him as I was of a mind to do it could have been the end of my Kingswood career.

The boys went peacefully to bed; I suppose some at least were rather regretting that I had not given one of their tormentors a good thumping. When I had calmed down, I went home and told Joyce. To my horror she suggested that I tell Dick Adams what I had done. Though I didn't think so at first, it was good advice. Within hours the story of my encounter with Phillip, suitably and graphically exaggerated in the telling, was all around the school. It would certainly, in due course, reach Adams's ears. I saw the headmaster and principal individually the next day to set the record straight. Bill Hall, the head, thought I had been quite restrained and Dick Adams's only remark was that he hoped I wouldn't be keeping order in the youth club like that.

Although I was not at all proud of my reaction to Phillip's jibe, it did me no harm with the boys or the staff. It passed into school folklore suitably embellished so that, in due course, new boys were warned not to push Stanners too far, "or you'll be for it!"

No sooner had the dust settled on this episode than I had another major and quite desperate crisis to face. The blow fell after a family weekend of unalloyed delight when we had a delightful trip around the countryside finishing at the seaside in glorious sun. On the Monday I went to do a usual duty getting the house up, and got a sense of impending doom when I noticed that boys with whom I thought I had developed a reasonable relationship were avoiding eye contact. What could be wrong? I found out when the head and deputy appeared together, the deputy to take over the house and the head to call me to his office for a chat. He did not beat about the bush.

"Kevin Johnson has made allegations about you – he says that you masturbated him in the house office last Friday. My clear instruction from the managers is that I have to investigate this to check the story so I must do so. What can you tell me?"

My faltering good spirits evaporated and, remembering Kevin's file and previous history, I felt a sick dread. I cast my mind back to Friday, when he had come to see me with a supposed problem.

"May I see you in private, Sir, in the housemaster's office?" Of course, if there was something he wanted to say.

"Could we close the door, Sir? I don't want some of the boys to see me."

I don't know what instinct for self-preservation possessed me, perhaps a memory of John's wise words after my first encounter with Kevin, but had replied, "The door stays open, I've to keep an eye on the house."

"So what did Kevin say?", I asked the headmaster.

"He says it was like the time he had run away, and you found him all wet and cold."

"Well I remember that – it's all written up in the file and in the log book." Thank you, John, my guardian angel.

The investigation was carried out swiftly and fairly. For a time I was desperately worried, but Kevin's story collapsed in ruins when three boys from Byron House, who happened to be in my class, came forward quite voluntarily to say that Kevin had been openly boasting that he was going to get Stanway and that he would then be one of Phillip's gang. Had Phillip or one of his mates put him up to it? We would never know. He finally admitted with bitter tears that it was all lies and that he had made up the story just to look big in the eyes of his mates.

Shocking as this incident was, there were definite pluses when I looked back on it. The first was the solid unwavering support of the staff. I had not realised I had such firm friends. John, in particular, was crystal clear in his account of Kevin's absconding and return. There was no possibility that Kevin's allegations could be true.

The second plus was the value of the whole episode as a learning experience, which stayed with me throughout my career in residential education. In retrospect, I must be grateful that the incident happened before the outbreak of political correctness, which decrees that all such allegations must be reported to the police. In the far off 1950s the guidance said that all allegations were to be investigated by the head and reported to the police unless the head was satisfied that the allegation was frivolous or malicious.

I was comforted by Joyce and I soon returned to planning what I hoped, was going to be a new and exciting development – a youth club in an approved school.

CHAPTER 3

A 'unique experiment'

As soon as I was cleared for normal duties again I set about planning for the youth club. I had confidently expected that all the preparation would be done in my own time and that I would continue to do full duties in Byron House, but to my complete astonishment Bill Hall said that, since I would obviously need some free time to prepare, I would be taken off house duties for a month starting after my next duty weekend in ten days time. I would like to think that this was a realistic assessment of the time needed but it may have been that he was simply weary of the constant upsets when Stanners was on duty. Whatever the motivation I experienced a dramatic lifting of spirits – life was worth living after all! Joyce, of course, took the news calmly. "It's no more than you deserve."

What other staff thought I could only guess at. Since the news about the youth club was not to be broadcast until plans were much further advanced and agreed by the managers, I imagine that the rumour mills were grinding away full blast.

"Stanners is on the way out."

"What's he done now?"

"Which one of the Approved School Rules has he broken?"

And so on.

Harry Worral, the relief teacher/instructor, was drafted in to take my form and to cover my house duties and I was despatched off home to get a plan together.

There was one aspect of the club which, for me, was non-negotiable: it must be self-governing, without a reliance on school discipline. Of course there would be the health and safety regulations applicable to any such organisation, but if we were to have any credence with boys we must not, *could* not rely on outside control. I had put this forward in the first discussion with Dick Adams and Bill Hall and it was greeted with scepticism and incredulity, particularly on the head's part. "What happens if they start smashing the place up? Wouldn't you send for me or the deputy?"

"If I had to then the club would effectively be finished. It must be self-regulating or we may as well not start."

After my disasters in Byron House I must have seemed either incredibly stupid or hell-bent on professional suicide. Of course there were apprehensions and worries, and I would wake in the small hours imagining all sorts of disasters, but there was also eager anticipation and I set about the planning without delay. Joyce agreed to type up the plans and deal with any correspondence on our ancient Remington and to keep my wilder flights of fancy in check, as least until the basic organisation was agreed.

The first step was to make contact with the local association of boys' clubs. There was, as was common in the 1950s, a flourishing local community of boys' clubs affiliated to the national association, the NABC. There was a full time local organiser, Tim Brightman, and a voluntary committee whose chairman, Sam Chapman, lived quite near the school. I met them together to explain what I had in mind and was delighted to find that they were supportive, even keen to help. Like all the other clubs in the district we would have to establish a voluntary management committee, pay a modest affiliation fee and agree to abide by the association rules. In return for these very modest requirements we would have access to local and national support and would be allowed to enter teams in the local boys' club leagues for football, cross county running, athletics and so on. I could hardly believe our good fortune.

As planning continued it became clear that we could not go further without the help and co-operation of staff – we had to go public. I broke the news at an after-lunch staff meeting to a very mixed reception. In particular there was a strong feeling among some staff that freedom from school discipline could only result in chaos. Perhaps they were right but there could be no turning back and, with Joyce's' help, I started to put flesh on the bare bones. Accommodation was easy: there was a suite of rooms next to the assembly hall ideal for the purpose. A large general room, a small room which could be fitted out as a kitchen, a separate room for a committee and an office. Much in need of decoration but that would be attended to.

The next priority was to get together a strong adult management committee and I was delighted when Sam Chapman agreed to add chairing of our committee to his district responsibilities. This was a priceless asset since he was in touch with all the local clubs and knew where there was surplus equipment we could beg or borrow. He was also a member of the local police committee and persuaded the police social club that a three-quarter size snooker table no longer being used could be passed over to us on permanent loan. Two full-size table tennis tables produced in the woodwork shop completed the main games facilities, supplemented by draughts, chess, shove ha'penny and a host of simple board games. More could be filled in when we were up and running.

The vacancies on the adult committee were filled in double quick time. The final line-up included two of the school managers, Brigadier Johnson and Miss Keen, a retired head-mistress well into her seventies but not at all fuddy-duddy. A local vicar and a prominent businessman completed the team. We had an initial meeting in our home, where Joyce produced tea and biscuits and was quizzed by the good Brigadier about her wartime experiences; somehow he had discovered that she had been bombed out of their London home before moving to Derbyshire.

Considerable scepticism was expressed about my insistence that we would not rely on school discipline. "What happens if they start to wreck the place?" Since I had no real idea, only half-formed and possibly half-baked plans for self government, leadership by example and the good influence of the Boys' Committee, I couldn't give any very sensible answers.

I made sure that Bill Hall and Dick Adams were kept fully up to date with developing plans and we had several useful joint discussions. I soon discovered that both men had had experience of voluntary work with youth clubs before they had entered the approved school field, and they had useful practical advice. The sticking point for Bill Hall was my insistence that I would not be calling on him or his deputy as a disciplinary backup if things were going wrong. In the end we agreed a compromise, mediated by Dick Adams, which would at least get the club up and running. My idea had been that I would let it be known from the beginning that the club would be self-governing. After considerable discussion I agreed that we would not announce it publicly as a policy until we were well established. Someone would be sure to test it out before self-government was beginning to work and the consequences for a fledgling organisation could be disastrous.

A more difficult issue to settle was the question of staff access to the club. For the teaching and house staff there was no problem – they would be welcome visitors at any time when the club was open – but for the head and his deputy there were difficulties. They were the two upon whom the disciplinary framework of the school mainly rested. They had the power, under Home Office rules, to administer corporal punishment and although this was strictly controlled and not frequently used it was an effective deterrent. When Bill Hall was doing his rounds of the school he did not need to raise his voice to establish order; peace came dropping slow. I knew instinctively that if he were to wander into a club evening the resultant calm would be due to his influence and not to any basic club ethos. With great generosity in view of my dismal record to date in Byron House, it was agreed that, for an experimental three-month period, neither Bill Hall nor Dick Adams would enter the club without a specific invitation from the Boys' Committee. Since at that stage we did not even have a committee and there was no indication as to who would be on it, this was risky as well as generous.

I wrote up a summary of our many discussions, which Joyce duly typed up, and with the approval of the powers that be – the senior staff, the school managers and the club management committee – it was in due course issued to staff as a confidential memo. At least it was supposed to be confidential but within days it was clear that it was common knowledge to the boys. We never discovered the source of the leak but in practical terms it mattered little since we were committed anyway.

My month of freedom from teaching and house duties passed all too quickly and the club's first session was duly scheduled. It was to be a short opening meeting at which I would detail some of the basic ideas behind the club. I explained that membership was open to any boy in the school who wished to join and who agreed to pay a weekly subscription of twelve pence in old money, or five new pence. There would be a Boys' Committee, selected by all the club members on a secret ballot. Nominations for committee members were to be put in writing. Boys had to agree to be nominated and the nomination had to be supported by at least a proposer and seconder. The committee would have six members, with at least one representative from each house. This meant that we had an election in two parts – a house ballot to choose one member from each house and a general school election to fill the three remaining places. I had toyed with the idea of using a proportional representation system but decided it was too complicated and settled on a simple first-past-the-post ballot.

Within two days nominations were completed and the papers handed in. One boy from each house, appointed by the housemaster, was to join me in going through the nomination papers to prepare for the two elections. With some apprehension I learned that among the Byron House nominees were Phillip and Raymond, the main architects of my difficulties in the house. In due course there was a list of eighteen candidates for the six places.

Ninety-three boys had signed up to join the club and eighty or so turned up for the election meeting. I duly explained that each member would have two votes – one for his house member and one for a general member. I got all eighteen nominated boys to stand up so that we could have a look at them and spent some time explaining the procedure for the secret ballot, which was to take place the following lunchtime in the club room. I had already invited two friends on the staff to oversee the election and ensure the fairness of the count, which the candidates would observe but could not take part in. The procedure, thanks to my good friend John, ran smoothly.

Ballot papers were issued with the names of all candidates and voting by cross or tick took place in two simply constructed polling booths. With such small numbers and supervision by experienced staff there was no problem with duplicate voting and in very short order the papers were collected from the ballot boxes and votes counted. I was somewhat dismayed, but certainly not surprised, to find that Phillip topped the poll for Byron House and that Raymond, his principal henchman, was third in the list for general membership. What did surprise me was that second place was occupied by Gary, a Byron House boy who had been considerably bullied but who had been one of the very few to show signs of revolt.

The final composition of the committee was very unbalanced since the three non-house representatives were all from Byron House. With four out of the six representatives from one house and Phillip and Raymond among them I could envisage a hard time to come. Perhaps if I'd thought more carefully I could have anticipated the result and arranged things differently but it was too late. The rules had been agreed, the election scrutineers had announced the results and for better or worse we were ready to start. I arranged to have our first committee meeting the next day and went home to give Joyce the bad news. If she was worried, she certainly did not show it. As usual she did her best to boost my self-confidence, but with so many memories of the humiliations Phillip and his gang had inflicted on me I was quite prepared for trouble.

The first hurdle to be got over was the election of a chairman for the Boys' Committee. After outlining what I expected the chairman to do I asked for volunteers. To my astonishment the only one of the six who declined to be considered was Phillip. What was he playing at? Some deep game no doubt, and my suspicions were confirmed when by four votes to one Raymond was voted in. I had a sick feeling that the battles of my first six months in Byron House were simply to be repeated in a different setting with Phillip pulling the strings and Raymond as his cat's-paw. The only consolation I could draw was that the two non-Byron boys and young Gary from Byron seemed keen to make things work. Norman from Carpenter House was anxious to know what powers the committee would have. I told them, in confidence, that in the end the whole existence of the club would rely on self-discipline since we would not be able to call in the head or the deputy to discipline unruly members.

"What can we do to them?", asked Norman.

"Well, like any boys' club we can stop membership."

"But what happens if those who aren't members come in anyway?"

I had no real idea, but I burbled on about it being up to me as club leader to deal with it and assured them that, with the committee support, we would manage. Raymond, already showing his authority as newly elected chairman, said, "There won't be any trouble if I'm there."

Why not, I wondered. Does that mean the same sort of trouble we had in Byron House? But this was not at all what Raymond had in mind. "I shall remind them what happened to Phillip when he insulted your wife, that'll cure them."

Should I have contradicted him and assured the committee that I had foresworn all violence? Maybe – but the committee agreed with Raymond and the moment passed.

I finished this first meeting by outlining some of the benefits we could expect from being members of a national organisation: competing in local leagues, using NABC camp sites, support for money raising events and so on. So far as the boys were concerned we finished on an optimistic note and we set about preparing for our opening night a week or so ahead. Posters were put up round the school, boys signed up for membership and the local NABC officials, Tim Brightman and Sam Chapman, were invited to the big send off.

It was a good job we didn't invite the whole adult committee as the evening was a fiasco. We had a grand total of eight boys at the club, including all of the committee. How embarrassing! Though Tim Brightman made encouraging noises, he must have wondered what the national association was letting itself in for. We had talked optimistically of breaking new ground in the approved school field, the harbinger of a new era in the treatment of juvenile delinquency, reform through self-discipline and self-control... I could have wept.

It was Phillip who struck an optimistic note. "They'll all be here tomorrow, just wait and see,"

"Why, what are you going to do? We can't force them in."

"It's not that, Sir, there's nothing worth watching on telly tomorrow." And so the mystery was explained – two of the houses had just installed new televisions and one of the local football teams was the featured match. Too late to explain as much to our visitors, who had long left.

The next night produced minor disasters of a different kind – such a crush of boys that our facilities were overwhelmed. We hastily arranged rotas for table tennis, snooker, table skittles and the like and repeatedly gave out board games, dominoes, draughts and chess. Some order was established but the best summary of the evening I could come up with was disorganised chaos. Worse was to come when we surveyed the shambles after the club was closed and the members had gone back to their houses. Only one of the six table tennis balls issued during the evening had been brought back, draughts and dominoes were scattered about and half the packs of cards which had been issued were now missing.

Fortunately there was a gap of three days over the weekend before the next club night and we had lengthy and detailed committee meetings to come to decide a plan of action. There was no shortage of ideas, some wildly impractical, but essentially we agreed on two lines of action. Firstly, the committee members agreed to monitor the way various equipment was given out and collected in. We would make it crystal clear to all members that if equipment was lost or broken it was members who suffered, since new equipment had to come from their subscriptions. To emphasise this we costed all the missing equipment in units of members' weekly subs. Thus a table tennis ball was one sub, a pack of cards four and a half subs, a table tennis bat six subs, and so on. Norman, the Carpenter House representative who was quite artistic, produced a large poster detailing all the losses of the first week.

At the same time we published a forward plan showing equipment we were hoping to buy in the future: new sports gear, some extra camping equipment, and – for the moment just a distant dream – angling gear and a sailing dinghy. Of course, the boys' subscriptions could not possibly cover the cost of all these items, but how could we persuade others to help us out if we could not even look after the stuff we had. One of the items that had caused most difficulty was the table tennis balls. They were trodden on, bashed against the walls or simply pocketed for use later in the houses. On little Gary's suggestion it was agreed that we should limit the number of balls to be issued during an evening to three per table. If a ball burst in fair play, it was to be given to the committee member responsible, who would replace it. There were many hurdles to be overcome and new difficulties to be faced, but after a couple of months we arrived at the point where equipment could be put out at the beginning of a club night in the sure knowledge that it would be treated properly and handed in, or checked over, intact at the end of the evening. We knew it was working when new members, unaware of the developing ethos, were taken to task by older members – "Eh, that's my subscriptions you're wasting. Cut it."

Effectively it meant that at any time during the evening we had thirty or forty boys watching to see that their money was not being wasted. Not perhaps the most altruistic of motives, but a useful lesson in civics nevertheless.

When I took stock of developments two months in I was reasonably satisfied, and for the first time since coming to Kingswood I was enjoying all aspects of my work: staffroom, schoolroom and now a flourishing and popular boys club. Fears expressed in many quarters about the disastrous effect of having no disciplinary intervention from school staff were not realised. There were some direct challenges to the authority of committee members and they needed support, but less than I had anticipated or feared. The real surprise was Gary, who had been considerably bullied in Byron House but was one of very few, perhaps the only one, who had refused to give way. His election demonstrated that he had won some respect from his peers for his uncompromising stand; what was more surprising was that, in the context of the club, he was well received by both Phillip and Raymond, his erstwhile tormentors.

Now that things were becoming more settled and I was more relaxed both in school and at home, I began to reconsider my approach in relation to Byron House boys and in particular Phillip and his two closest supporters, Raymond and Tim. I began by making a more detailed study of the files of all the boys in the house, and of the boys from the other houses who were now becoming more involved in club activities, than had been possible when I had been under so much pressure. The details were shattering. I had never imagined such a catalogue of misery, hardships and in many cases sheer cruelty. Not in all cases of course – some boys had a relatively simple history of truanting, shoplifting, stealing and eventually, generally after several court appearances, Approved School Orders. These could be called the straightforward cases. But the six youngsters who were now, for better or worse, the leaders of the youth club were in a different category.

I began my more detailed study by sifting through the voluminous file of Phillip. I knew the basic facts, that he was illegitimate and had been adopted by well-meaning but somewhat elderly parents who already had a fifteen-year-old daughter. It was not immediately clear from the file why they had decided in their forties to adopt Phillip, but I came across a paragraph written by Phillip and included without comment. He had clearly been asked at some stage to summarise his history, and the bitterness showed – "I was the result of a one night stand between a prostitute and a GI. Abandoned in a church Children's Home and picked up by 'do it yourself' marriage councillors in a church rummage sale."

Not at all a fair summary. His mother was not a prostitute but in the fashion of the times had been shunted by her parents into a mother and baby home and persuaded that adoption was the best and probably, in the circumstances, the only possible outcome. The adoptive parents, comfortably settled in a pleasant suburb, gave what support they could to Phillip but were baffled by his continued delinquencies and his apparently total rejection of their high standards. The sister, now married and with family of her own, kept sporadically in touch with Phillip but was clearly losing patience with him.

As I read more deeply I began to see Phillip with new eyes, as an intelligent but deeply disturbed youngster tormented by demons from his past which he could not exorcise. With the minimal contact I had with the young man there was no way I could think of helping, but at least I would show him understanding. I noted that he had been recommended for psychiatric help but that after just two interviews with the visiting consultant psychiatrist there had been no further contact because Phillip had forcefully and categorically refused to see someone he scornfully dismissed as 'the Nut Doctor'. My own relationship with Phillip had subsided into an uneasy but no longer uncomfortable truce, so perhaps, just perhaps, there was some understanding on both sides.

Raymond's history was quite different. His parents were divorced; father had custody and had remarried. The stepmother was the archetypal wicked witch, who apparently resented the relationship between father and son and lost no opportunity to make it clear to Raymond. He had received little love, some ill treatment when he was younger and a series of stand-up rows when he became too big for her to hit. There was a suggestion, unproven and not followed up, of sexual abuse and it now seemed most unlikely that he had any future with father, who would hear nothing said against his wife. There had been efforts to establish contact with his natural mother but so far these had come to nothing. The latest treatment plans suggested independent living with continuing support from after-care agencies.

Sam, the third Byron House boy, was a more straightforward case. Like numbers of others he was essentially the product of his home environment. The youngest of seven children, by the time he was born his mother, still in her early thirties, was pretty well worn out by the incessant demands of her children and receiving very little help from her husband, who seemed to be on permanent sickness benefit. Perhaps the most hopeful sign was that, after a hysterectomy, mother was at last taking a more active role in the house, while one older brother and sister were not only contributing financially but were helping to look after the younger children. I visited the household with Sam and though it was somewhat chaotic there was obviously a lot of love. Sam seemed well accepted and was obviously proud of his new responsibilities as a club committee member. He was delighted to talk about the work he was doing and his new-found responsibility in ensuring equipment wasn't damaged.

Gary, the fourth Byron House boy, was one of the very few who had shown any signs of standing up to Phillip and his cronies. He had been bullied for his pains but, so far as I could tell, had never completely given in to Phillip's demands. At the same time he had not been co-operative with me while I was on house duties. However, in the freer atmosphere of the club he was beginning to blossom and was winning the respect of his fellow committee members. Though not at all academic, he was full of bright ideas for club development and more than willing to do his share of setting out equipment, watching over it and then coping with tidying up and checking off at the end of the evening. His history could be said to be that typical of many approved schoolboys. A long history of truancy, shop lifting, joy riding in stolen – or at least 'borrowed' – cars and eventually the more serious offences of robbery and then burglary. Dad had long deserted the family and a series of 'uncles' coming and going in the home added nothing in the way of stability. His treatment plan, as for Raymond, envisaged independent living with long term after-care support.

Norman, the Carpenter House boy, was the second of six children and had a tragic family history. Father had been killed in a motorbike accident just after the birth of the youngest child and mother had died of cancer two years before Norman came to us. The two girls were being cared for by an aunt in Birmingham, and were said to be as happily settled as could be expected in the circumstances. The four boys, ages ranging from six to nineteen, were continuing to be cared for by Gordon, the eldest son, who had given up work for the purpose and was being supported financially and practically with regular home care by the social services department. It was apparently working well for the younger boys but not for Norman, who resented his brother's authority and was very soon getting into various kinds of trouble with the authorities. He was sent to a remand home for a month for reports but found the regime there much more to his liking than his home. When he returned home after the month he was quickly in further trouble. He was committed to an approved school when Gordon went to court with him and admitted that, though he loved Norman, he could not cope with him in the home. At Kingswood, Norman was well settled in the school, was making good academic progress and had ambitions to join the Royal Navy. He clearly enjoyed both the club activities and the responsibilities he was given as a committee member.

Gerald, the Wesley House boy, was an enigmatic character. The only child of parents who were described as 'loving and supportive' he had been anti-authority and difficult even in primary school, and when he reached secondary school was in frequent rows with staff and his fellow pupils. He was assessed by the county psychologist as above average intelligence, but she could find no clue as to his aberrant behaviour. He came to approved school in the end after his day school lost patience with his aggressive behaviour and the police charged him with a whole series of thefts and driving offences. He was receiving detailed help from our resident clinical psychologist and appeared to be making progress. The parents kept in regular contact and were delighted that at last someone seemed to be getting through to Gerald. School staff, well aware of false dawns with similar boys in the past, were cautiously optimistic but quite prepared for trouble ahead.

This, then, was the team which was to be the driving force for the exciting new venture in an approved school, a club which could function without the direct support of school discipline. Not at all a bad group – committee meetings were constructive and forward looking. We planned with growing optimism for the winter season when the club would be entering at least one team in the local NABC football leagues and we were actively considering a range of other activities with local clubs.

In this mood of positive planning we booked our NABC campsite in the Mendips for a weekend away in mid-July, six weeks ahead, and started a range of competitive tables for table tennis, snooker, billiards and chess. All seemed to be set fair and the next time Tim Brightman and Sam Chapman visited for an informal club evening everything seemed to be running like clockwork. There was no hint of any disasters lurking around the corner: the club was well attended, equipment was generally well cared for, and there were no more than the minor squabbles usual with a group of active adolescent schoolboys. I even found time to do lesson preparation on club evenings.

I was particularly pleased with Gerald. Described by a club leader from his parents' church, who had made a valiant effort to capture Gerald's interest, as 'unclubbable, aggressive, antisocial and disruptive', he was now using his organising talents and undoubted intelligence to good effect in organising and running 'ladder' tournaments for snooker and billiards. The separate room, which housed two tables, was a haven of peace and quiet without even the ubiquitous rock and roll that blasted through the main clubroom. Little Gary did give me some veiled hints that Gerald needed watching but he was entirely non-specific and I put it down to inter-house jealousy.

The sword of Damocles fell when a police car drew up at the main school entrance and two officers emerged with a firm grip on two boys who were supposed to be in the snooker room but had been caught stealing from a local house. Although this concerned club boys it could not, since the police were involved, be dealt with as a purely club matter. The head used his well practised and effective interrogation methods and the truth soon emerged. Not really difficult since the pair had been caught red-handed by a muscular householder.

If it had been one robbery, with two boys involved, we could have lived with it fairly comfortably. An apology to the householder, a police caution for the boys – who were anyway already subject to an Approved School Order – and the offence, serious as it was, would be dealt with as a routine school matter. As the investigation went on, however, it became clear that there were serious ramifications centred on Gerald. Indeed, he seemed to be the mastermind behind a considerable operation.

The procedure started with Gerald, out in the district with a legally obtained Saturday pass, investigating suitable properties to be raided. He then instructed some of his cronies in simple ways of getting into the property. Working in pairs, the smarter of the two was told to knock at the door while his mate kept watch. If someone answered he had some ready excuse, carefully tutored by Gerald. If no one came they were to go round the back, where in almost every case they would find the small top window in the toilet or bathroom open. No problem for two active boys to clamber up, open the main window and get in. Upstairs to the main bedroom and very often in the top drawers of the dressing table they would find money. Don't, under any circumstances, they were instructed, take it all. Take a few pounds; if there's fifty, take ten or fifteen. Leave everything else untouched, go carefully downstairs and boldly go out of the front door. Back to school, in by one of the many back ways in known to boys and back to the snooker table. Gerald would cover their absence and share in the proceeds of the robberies. When investigations were complete it turned out that seven different houses had been raided in the space of a fortnight; only one had reported a theft to the police. The rest had either not noticed or perhaps wives had blamed husbands or vice versa.

My naïvety was humiliating. There were predictably some staff members ready to say, "I told you so. It could never work the way Stanway wanted it." Others were more sympathetic, taking the line that it could have happened to anyone but asking how we were going to ensure it didn't happen again. Whatever conclusions we might decide on as a club there could be no question of it remaining entirely an internal matter. At the very least, the police would expect the boys to appear in our local juvenile court. The local residents, supportive as they generally were to the school, would have harsh things to say if they did not see any action. We called an urgent committee meeting, minus Gerald, who was unavailable anyway being confined to his house, and had a long and serious discussion.

As I pointed out, the immediate problem was out of our hands. In a very short time, seven boys who had been duly charged with theft or, in Gerald's case, receiving would appear in court. They would almost certainly be returned to the school, suitably lectured and warned by the magistrates – since they were already subject to Approved School Orders there was little more the court could do. The boys were all too young to be sent for Borstal training, fines would be a meaningless exercise and community service a non-starter. The school would give what assurances it could about their future conduct and then pick up the threads. There would have to be restitution of the money stolen, and the culprits would be expected to apologise personally as the money was given back. Astonishingly, most of the money stolen had not been spent but had been carefully hidden pending a major share out at the next home leave. Gerald had been astute enough to realise that any unusually large spending locally would immediately give the game away.

Up to that point the decisions were simple, but what would happen after the court appearance? Should the boys be allowed back in the club and if so under what conditions? Should Gerald still be on the committee? There were also other urgent matters to settle – we could no longer assume that because boys had told house staff they were going to the club that they would actually be there. The golden rule about evening activities in the school was that staff, including me as club leader, had to know where boys were. The halcyon early days of the club had to be modified. Discussion raged!

It was most interesting to me to watch the developing dynamic among the five remaining committee members. Phillip had the most aggressive outlook: "Kick them all out for good, we're better off without them." Norman, from Carpenter House, used to a well run and orderly set-up, agreed with Phillip. Sam and Gary were much more conciliatory, not, I suspected, from any strong feelings on the matter, but because they were enjoying the feeling of opposing Phillip. The real surprise to me was Raymond. With a maturity I had not expected he led the discussion with patience and a degree of tact, as well as a quite surprising grasp of the club principles we had set out. If the club was to mean anything we had to keep our independence from school discipline.

It soon became clear that we had a clear split, with Norman and Phillip adamantly in favour of throwing the book at all seven miscreants and Gary and Sam, whatever their motives, supporting Raymond in taking a softer line. I was careful not to come down too strongly on either side – self government had to mean something – but I did ask if they knew what Gerald was saying around the school. None of them knew so I suggested they should find out before the next day when we would have another meeting.

Before that there was yet another surprising development; Joyce found a letter from Gerald pushed through our front door, addressed to her and marked 'Private'. It contained three pound notes with a letter of apology and explanation. It was literate and the spelling correct. The letter was quite long but the gist was that when we had had a committee meeting in our house Gerald had taken the opportunity to steal three pounds from Joyce's handbag.

> *You trusted me to bring in tea and biscuits and left your handbag in the kitchen. I let you down and I'm sorry, this is all the money I stole. Please forgive me.*

Joyce had thought that the housekeeping had not lasted well that week but had not realised the cash had been stolen. She showed me the letter and said she thought it was quite genuine. "After all," she said, "no one knew he had stolen the money. He didn't need to say anything."

I remembered his file – the long history of stealing, including from his parents. I recalled his plausibility, his repeated pleas to his parents for forgiveness, only to let them down again and again. I could think of several less honourable reasons for the letter: three pounds could perhaps be a small price for him to pay if it put him back into Stanway's good books. But Joyce thought I was being much too cynical. What harm would there be if we took the letter at face value and gave him fresh chances?

"In any case I've got to thank him for the letter and for returning the money. Could I see him?"

I could think of no good reason why not and with the approval of the housemaster and John Briers, the psychologist, she duly had a long and, in her view, useful session with Gerald in the school interview room. She had thought it might be less formal to conduct the conversation at home, but no doubt she would soon put Gerald at his ease – it was a gift she possessed in abundance, a natural empathy with difficult youngsters. She became convinced that Gerald was genuinely sorry and suggested that at least we should give him the chance to talk to the committee.

At this stage I deemed it prudent to put Dick Adams and Bill Hall in the picture – it was, after all, their school and their heads on the line if there was trouble with the locals. They were both more supportive than I had the right to expect in view of the clear mistakes I had already made in organisation. I assured them that we would ensure better recording of boys' whereabouts so that if they were outside the school without permission we would at least know about it. Bill Hall made it clear that there could be no interference with police procedures and that the school management committee would need to be fully informed. I was grateful that we had influential and supportive managers on the club's adult committee.

With some reluctance but with Raymond's clear support as our chairman, the Boys' Committee agreed to hear what Gerald had to say for himself and what assurances he might give for his future conduct. I dropped a few hints to individual members as to various possibilities, including the possibility that Gerald might suggest his own punishment. This was a technique which I tried out with some success in the youth club I had run in Derbyshire and I was curious to see what Gerald, confirmed delinquent as he was, would come up with. We had little to lose: all the various punishments the majesty of the law could devise had had no visible effect, nor had the sanctions imposed by his increasingly despairing parents.

With only minimal help from me, Raymond organised the meeting. Gerald was told to sit on a straight-backed chair on one side of the largest table we had in the club. Each committee member had paper and a pencil in front of him to take notes and Raymond opened the proceedings by saying that he had heard that boys had sneaked out of the club and done some stealing in the district and that Gerald had taken part. He then straight away invited Gerald to give his version of events. Gerald began truthfully by saying he had not done any stealing himself.

"Oh, didn't you? Are you saying you had nothing to do with it? Surely since you were in charge of snooker you must have known something was going on. What did you think the boys who were missing were doing?"

"Well, I didn't really know, they could have been going for a walk."

"Really Gerald, you didn't know?!" A scornful sneer. "Shall we get Peter and David to come in and give us their stories?"

Clearly Raymond was building up to a dramatic climax. He had the full facts, he had witnesses, and he was enjoying Gerald's obvious twisting and turning. I could see echoes of all the police and school interrogations Raymond had endured in the past and made a mental note to have another look at his police record.

How long it would have taken Raymond to get to the truth we would never know for suddenly, out of the blue, Gary decided to take a hand.

"Cut the crap Gerald, and tell the truth, we all know it anyway. You set it all up and shared the money. Stop giving us a load of bull."

"All right, Gary, you've had your say, let somebody else have a go. What have you got to say, Norman?"

"Same as Gary, tell him to get on with it – we're just wasting time."

"Okay Gerald, you've heard Gary and Norman. Now start again and tell us the truth, the whole truth, and nothing but the truth." More echoes of past interviews.

With staff, or police, or parents, Gerald might well have continued to lie, but in front of his peers he knew that was a complete waste of time and he soon told us the whole story, including some bits that Bill Hall and the police did not know. Some useful comments on house security, and details of where the money had been found. He assured us that none of the money stolen had so far been spent.

"Oh yes it has," said Phillip, who had his own impeccable sources of information. "You don't really think that Peter and Gordon" – two of the culprits from Byron House – "actually had their own money to buy all those cigarettes?"

This evidence of falling out among thieves was clearly a body blow to Gerald, whose self-confidence was rapidly ebbing away. Backed into a corner by his ruthless interrogators, who were clearly enjoying the sensation of for once being on the side of the law, Gerald gave a clear and lucid account of all the thefts, including his own stealing from Joyce. This last admission drew some acid comments from the committee, most particularly and most surprisingly from Phillip. It became clear that his comment that Joyce was a "fucking prostitute" was not at all his real assessment of her. Joyce and her family were for him the embodiment of what family life should be like. Perhaps she represented his dream of the mother he had never known and whom he had scornfully dismissed in writing as a prostitute. I registered his reaction and noted that, unlikely as it had appeared during my disastrous months as deputy housemaster, there might be an opening to get through to this intelligent but difficult boy.

When the full story had emerged and been certified as correct in every detail by Phillip, the committee looked for guidance as to what punishments should be given. At this point Raymond came up with the sensible suggestion that Gerald should leave the room while the committee considered what was to be done. There was no shortage of suggestions, mostly wildly impossible to enforce without involving school discipline.

"Just kick him out of the club," said Norman, with enthusiastic endorsement from Sam. "We're better off without him."

It was Raymond who proposed, as I had planted in his mind, that we should hear what Gerald had to say about his own punishment. After some hesitations and to the considerable disgust of Norman and Sam, who were relishing the thought of being executioners, it was agreed that we should at least ask Gerald. He was accordingly called back in with due ceremony and put on the spot. Somewhat to my surprise he began with an impassioned plea to be allowed to remain a club member.

"I'll do anything – clean up the club, do the washing up, sweep the yard, whatever – I've got to go to court anyway and they'll probably send me to Borstal." I didn't tell him he was too young for Borstal, though when I thought about it afterwards I was pretty sure he knew anyway. He was both streetwise and intelligent.

Whether it was the thought of getting out of cleaning chores or whether it was genuine sympathy for Gerald, the committee, by three votes to two, agreed with Gerald's suggestions. The only question to be settled was the timescale. Norman wanted a year, the others six months. In the end it was agreed we should try it for a month and then review progress.

What was clear was that Gerald was no longer acceptable to the rest of the Boys' Committee, or for that matter to me, as a committee member and we therefore set in motion the procedure for selecting a new member. It was to be someone from Wesley House and we left it to the house to make the selection. There were four nominations from the forty boys and in a straightforward first-past-the-post secret ballot the outright clear winner was Darrell Hampstead. We could have anticipated the result, as Darrell was a bright, intelligent, physically attractive youngster, good at all sports, strong but not a bully and in all respects well liked by both staff and his peers. Unfortunately, from my point of view, his record of conduct in the fourteen months he had been in the school was dismal. He had already absconded half a dozen times and had committed a series of offences – burglary, shop lifting, taking and driving away and at least one case of fraud involving a stolen chequebook. Were we to lose Gerald only to replace him with an even more sophisticated thief?

I had no contact with Darrell in the house and very little in school, since he was on the woodwork department and I therefore saw him only on a Wednesday. Not always then, even, as his classroom work was so well up to standard that if he had urgent work in progress in the woodwork shop he would be excused his studies. When he was in class I found him co-operative and helpful. So what were the influences which were driving him to such anti-social behaviour? I turned to his file for clues and was quite devastated to read his history. His mother had deserted the home when he was a toddler, no doubt as a reaction to her treatment by her husband who, by all accounts, was quite violent at times, particularly when he had had too much to drink. Father had married again but the stepmother was, according to report, quite abusive and violent towards Darrell. There was a suggestion of sexual abuse, which had been reported by the school to social services. The only result, so far as Darrell was concerned, was that father supported stepmother in her denials and gave Darrell a good hiding for telling lies!

The situation was complicated by the fact that whenever social services visited the home both parents presented a united front, loving and caring for each other and for a younger half sister of Darrell's who was, to all intents and purposes, doing well at school and living happily at home. There was at least one report in the file which cast doubt on all Darrell's allegations and stated that this intelligent boy was quite capable of inventing stories to break up the marriage. He did have some contact with his natural mother and though it was generally agreed that there was no possibility of him living with her it remained his clear aim.

Darrell's home background would not in any way affect his capability to be a good committee member in the eyes of the other boys. He was universally popular with club members. I had no legitimate grounds for over-ruling the Wesley House choice, and no reason to believe that any other of the nominees would be better, but I needed to be sure that Darrell would not be leading others astray as far as absconding and stealing were concerned. I decided to seek the opinions of those who knew him best: the Wesley House staff and our psychologist John Briers. Without reservation they recommended him to the club. I ran into unexpected opposition, however, from Bill Hall.

"You're surely not going to allow it!"

"I don't see how I can stop it," I replied. "Darrell has been properly elected in accordance with agreed Boy's Club procedure."

"But you could have vetoed his nomination."

In an increasingly acrimonious discussion, the head detailed Darrell's appalling record of absconding and offending. Eventually he concluded that Darrell's appointment would be such a clear signal to the other boys that serial delinquencies brought reward and not punishment that it simply could not be allowed. I argued further but had the good sense not to push Bill into a corner. He was a good headmaster, who had to date given me solid support in establishing the club, but I was well aware of his reservations and, indeed, could see some logic in them. If I pressed him too far he would veto Darrell's appointment.

I was left in a quandary. To what extent should I dig in my heels? Did it really matter if I abandoned this small principle and went along with him? I temporised by saying that I would give the matter more thought and went home to consult with Joyce. She was horrified.

"It will be disastrous for Darrell on top of everything he has had to put up with in life. You've got to stand firm!"

"But Bill has got a point. Darrell is a disaster area!"

"And that's why we've got to do something positive."

But what if we succeeded in getting Darrell appointed and then had a repeat of the disaster with Gerald? What if he took other boys with him on his next absconding? What if he used his intelligence and popularity to corrupt the club? All these theoretical considerations counted little with Joyce, who could only see the needs of a desperately troubled boy.

Bill Hall and I had reached an impasse but fortunately we had another of our regular briefings with Dick Adams. To my considerable astonishment it became clear that Adams was fully in the picture over the Darrell saga and he took the initiative to resolve matters. "I gather we've a problem over the appointment of a new club committee member. Is it true that the boys want Darrell Hampstead?"

"Well yes. They've voted overwhelmingly for him."

"That must be a problem. Isn't he the one whose been running away and committing offences all over the place. Can we really have him in such a position of responsibility? The Home Office Inspectorate will support us if we give the go-ahead – they think that giving boys this sort of responsibility is a brilliant experiment, something unique in an approved school – but what do you think, Bill?"

This was a superb ploy on Dick Adams part. He had made it clear that the Home Office would be in favour, the inference that he himself was in favour was quite clear, and yet he had in no way undermined Bill Hall's authority. The ball was back in the head's court.

The atmosphere thawed. Bill Hall found himself agreeing not only that Darrell's appointment could go ahead but that if it succeeded it would be a triumph for the school as well as the club. And if it failed? Then the opprobrium would be on my shoulders and not Bill Hall's.

CHAPTER 4

The club gathers ground

With the clear recognition that it was my neck on the line, I took every chance to chat with Darrell. The gist of what was said was quite simple – he very much wanted to be a committee member because he liked the club and enjoyed organising things. What about his absconding and stealing, what did he have to say about this? Was he prepared to make any promises for the future?

"No, Sir, I can't. When the mood takes me I have to go."

"What about the other boys?"

"I can promise you about them, Sir. I would never take anyone with me – they have asked and I have always said no."

"What do you tell them when you are brought back to school?"

"I tell them what a fool I've been and that it's not worth it."

"You do know that you've already lost three days home leave and that if it happens again you could lose the rest."

"That would be good, Sir."

I had a vivid glimpse of the dark despair behind that statement – it was a revelation. This was an honest assessment of a bleak, barren home situation. My heart ached for this intelligent, gifted boy with such a hopeless future. And what of the other allegations he had made about his stepmother, were they true also? At that stage in my career I was quite naïve about sexual abuse. I could just about get my mind around abuse of a child by a man, but a woman sexually abusing a thirteen-year-old, and a stepmother at that? Not possible. It must be, as visitors to the home had hinted, a nasty slur on a caring wife who was doing her best. A cunning ploy to break up a hated marriage. And yet this unhappy boy was coming across to me as genuine and honest. For the time being I set aside my doubts and reservations as 'awaiting further enlightenment' and welcomed Darrell on to the committee. At the earliest opportunity I went back to his file and read the detailed reports on his abscondings, including the copies of police reports. They all followed a similar pattern.

Leaving the school was, of course, not a problem. The boys were not locked in. At that time there was not even night super-vision other than an occasional walk round the dormitories by senior staff or some single member of staff having a look round before going to bed. No problem then for a determined boy to leave in the early morning hours, walk to the nearest main road and thumb a lift. By the time his absence was discovered when staff came on duty at 7am he could be miles away.

So far as Darrell was concerned it did not matter what direction he was taken, and as soon as he was, in his view, far enough away from school to be at least temporarily safe he would purchase breakfast in some convenient café, using money he had carefully hoarded, and then he would set out to steal. Whether he had picked up the technique from Gerald and his compan-ions or whether it was just general knowledge, his *modus operandi* was very similar. Find a respectable, middle-class district, check that the chosen house was empty, gain entry as unobtrusively as possible and take whatever money could be found. The differ-ence between Gerald's gang and Darrell was that Darrell would happily take all he could find. He had absolutely no qualms about the thefts being discovered. He would then put forty or fifty miles or so between him and the crime scene, this time travelling by coach or train, before settling in at some guest house or small hotel with a plausible story about being on a walking holiday and needing a few days rest. He had a rucksack and equipment to bolster his story and was sufficiently tall and well set up to pass as seventeen, or eighteen.

Four or five days later – perhaps a week – he would go to the nearest police station and give himself up. In quick time he would be reported to the school and a member of staff would be despatched to collect him. No difficulty raised by Darrell: any member of staff could collect him without fear of him being difficult or running away. Back to the head for punishment, certainly loss of privileges and probably three or four strokes on the bottom with an Approved Home Office cane, all duly recorded and accepted by Darrell without demur.

It was quite clear from reading the various accounts, all remarkably similar, that these were the exploits of a talented, deeply troubled boy with a specific personal agenda. There was never any violence, and when the police questioned him about his offences he gave them careful and accurate accounts detailing exactly what he had taken and even the street names and addresses. The school's dilemma was how his talent might be redirected into non-antisocial pursuits. It was clear that if we did not do it soon he would be of an age to go to Borstal; when that day arrived the police would insist on taking him to court and with his lengthening crime record he would be removed from our care. Perhaps, after all, it was good to have him on the club committee. Just maybe we could give him a new purpose in life.

In due course we reported all the changes including the appointment of Darrell to the club committee to Dick Adams and Bill Hall. The head was understandably still dubious about Darrell. "Will he not just take advantage of the club situation to abscond again?"

"Well, he hasn't promised not to run away again, but he has said he won't let the club down by either running away from the club or taking any club members with him."

My two senior colleagues agreed it was worth a trial and at the same time I assured them that in future we would initiate a more efficient checking system. The houses were to send us lists each club evening of those who were attending, and I agreed to see that they did not wander off without my express permission.

And so normal service was resumed, with a special eye on the snooker room. We were nearing the next home leave period, the Whitsuntide holiday, twelve months since my first encounter with Kingswood as an invited guest. Then I had enjoyed the experience of a small group of boys in relaxed circumstances and with no hint of the desperate struggles to come. Since then I had survived my final six months in Derbyshire, four months of battles royal and disasters in Byron House, a month of preparation for the new club venture and the last few weeks' experience of running the club, with its minor triumphs and major upsets. The jury was still out as to our success or failure, but having broken up Gerald's Mafia we had some genuine grounds for optimism. We were actively planning some camping weekends away, the football season was ahead and we had already optimistically entered teams for the local boys' club league. Before that we were to have a family holiday in Scotland.

We were already experienced campers and proud owners of an ex-army tent of such heavy canvas that when it was fastened up we were in Stygian blackness. It was very heavy and bulky but too small for our growing family so we replaced it with a larger, up-to-the-minute lightweight tent. We loaded our primitive but efficient Primus stoves and cooking equipment into the Ford Popular, put cases, chairs and a collapsible table on the roof rack and set off full of enthusiasm. A few days with our families in Derbyshire *en route* and then off up the A1 to Scotland. We pitched camp just over the border near Berwick-on-Tweed, and cooked a meal. Then the heavens opened – but not to worry, we had a brand new tent...

"Daddy, we're getting wet" said Kate.

"Don't worry, it's just a little mist, the new canvas weathering."

If only we had kept our old, entirely weatherproof tent. We decamped to the car and waited impatiently for dawn while our daughters slept peacefully on the back seat. At first light we surveyed the wreckage of our bedding and left to find a transport café for refuge and a hot meal. We struggled on through torrential rain to somewhere north of Perth and then – campers' heaven! – found a site with a splendid, comfortable, modern four-berth caravan for hire. The buxom landlady took pity on the bedraggled pair (Joyce and me, that is, not the children: they were warm and comfortable on the back seat), welcomed us into her home and gave us hot drinks. We paid for a week's hire of the caravan and began the forlorn job of unpacking our sodden equipment. Just as we were finishing, a watery sun struggled through the clouds. We had no more rain until we packed up a week later.

We had a wonderful time. Joyce had just recently passed her driving test and took to the narrow highland roads as to the manner born. She coped competently when a magnificent stag dashed out in front of the car and she grew in confidence daily. Of course, in the 1950s traffic was negligible compared to today. We saw all the usual sights of central and lowland Scotland, parked without any difficulty in Princes Street in Edinburgh, traversed the Trossachs, took a trip on Loch Lomond and admired the Caledonian Canal and the glorious Highlands. We returned home refreshed in body and spirit, with none of the dread on my part of a few months previously. In my absence the club had been closed for a week after the boys' home leave, and as we stopped outside our house to unpack we were approached by a group of boys offering to help us unpack and wanting to know when the club was going to be open. I gave them the date, four days hence, but before that I had been asked to meet the head and principal to report on the first two months' operations of the club and to discuss requirements for the future.

I was somewhat apprehensive, remembering the disastrous unplanned evening class in housebreaking not to mention the debacle of our opening night. There were good things to report, however: we were getting to grips with looking after the equipment, and the club was well attended. I also felt that we had established the principle that we did not have to rely on the school disciplinary procedures sufficiently well for it to continue with no modification other than the undertaking we had already given to keep an unobtrusive check on the boys' whereabouts.

My senior colleagues expressed satisfaction with progress and made light of the depredations in the district by Gerald's gang. It helped that the boys had done no physical damage to property, that all the money had been returned (including some that house-holders had not even missed) and that all the boys involved had given polite apologies to all concerned. It was an episode in the school's history which could be recorded and set aside, though I would always remember it as a sharp learning experience.

I was asked whether there were any other resources I needed for the future. Emboldened by what I could see was a favour-able atmosphere I said that if the club was to develop to its full extent I would need some extra adult help. This could be amply justified by the number of boys the club occupied each night it was open. There were pluses and minuses involved: some of the voluntary evening activities run by other staff as part of their extraneous duties – chess clubs, music group, gym games, and so on – had seen a falling off in attendance. I had not heard staff complaining, as smaller groups were more easily managed and could allow for more detailed and useful individual work. But it did mean that in terms of boy-hours I was doing more than my share. I put these points forward as delicately as possible, while making it clear that I was not complaining at the amount of work but only looking at ways we could work more effectively.

Bill Hall suggested that we might simply incorporate some of the regular evening activities into the club programme and that staff who were willing could work in the club. I rejected this possibility outright. It was not that I distrusted my colleagues or would scorn the co-operation; it was simply a gut feeling that bringing in staff who already operated through the day in a disciplinary framework would gradually, but inevitably, alter the pattern of the club. The need was recognised – a good step forward – but the best we could come up with was to recruit voluntary unpaid help from outside the school.

There was one further point that I wished to make clear. In the initial setting up of the club, in order to be independent of school discipline Dick Adams and Bill Hall had agreed to stay out of the club unless they had been specifically invited. This voluntary and much appreciated limiting of their responsibility had been a vital step in getting it across to boys that we were a genuine organisation. However, now that we were well established I felt we had reached the point where we could welcome visits from senior staff on an informal basis without upsetting our basic philosophy.

These two decisions – to try to recruit voluntary staff and to accept senior staff visits – were to have far reaching consequences for the club and for my future which I certainly did not envisage at the time. I went home, not discouraged but having no idea how I could recruit voluntary unpaid staff, and as usual poured out all my worries to Joyce. To my astonishment she said, "Well you've got one volunteer straight away. I'll come."

"How can you manage that?"

She had it all off pat. We already had a regular babysitter, Lyn, the daughter of one of our housemasters. She came when our two daughters were in bed and did her homework while we had a precious evening out.

"She'll welcome a bit of extra pocket money for another evening."

And so she did. She was completely reliable and good with the children, who were no trouble anyway and loved Lyn to bits. Joyce had already passed the Home Office checks for all staff, since she had contact with the club committee boys when we had meetings at home, and so with the ready approval of Bill Hall and Dick Adams she was duly recruited and installed as our first unpaid volunteer. I cleared it with the club committee, who welcomed the idea with enthusiasm.

We did not make any formal announcement – it was not necessary. On the second night of our re-opening Joyce simply wandered in, joined in a game of Ludo with little Gary and was soon at home. Before her first night was over she had somehow persuaded Phillip to have a game of chess. She was not fond of the game and was very much a novice, but when I looked in the room Phillip was patiently explaining some of the standard endings and Joyce was listening in apparently rapt attention, as though it was all new to her. I didn't interrupt!

The next time Joyce appeared for a session Phillip approached her with a diffident shyness most unusual for him to ask if she wanted another game. They duly disappeared into the small committee room, but when I looked in shortly afterwards the game had hardly progressed at all. The two of them were deep in conversation.

"What on earth were you nattering about?", I asked later.

"We weren't nattering, he was telling me about his mum. He said she'd be thirty-two now. That's a year older than me."

"Cor, that means she could look like you," Phillip had responded, making mental comparisons between Joyce and his adoptive mother, now in her fifties and showing her age. Joyce said she could see Phillip making these readjustments and taking a new view of things.

"I do hope I haven't spoilt things between him and his adoptive mum."

That was not very likely — relationships between them had been pretty disastrous for years. We could only wait to see what developed but I did suggest that Joyce should at least talk to our psychologist to put him in the picture. John was interested, but quite reassuring. He thought it good that this troubled youngster was establishing a relationship with an adult. Phillip was obviously seeing Joyce as a prototype for the mother he had never known. John did warn Joyce against getting too involved too emotionally. Good advice generally but Joyce couldn't see it so far as Phillip was concerned. Someone, she thought, had to get close to the boy.

For my part, I was not entirely comfortable with Joyce's approach. I remembered the apparent venom with which Phillip had called her a "fucking prostitute" and how it had come near to finishing my approved school career, but Joyce had taken it lightly at the time and obviously bore Phillip no malice. "Perhaps we'll discuss it sometime, perhaps not, it doesn't matter."

In fact it was Phillip who eventually brought it up over the chessboard.

"Did you— have you— were you ever told what I called you, Mrs S? You know, when Stanners lost his rag?"

"Well I'm not sure if I remember exactly what you said. What was it?"

"Oh, you know, I called you one of those—"

"One of what?"

"Those women that do it for money!"

"Oh, you mean prostitutes. That wasn't very nice of you was it?"

"No it wasn't – I wish I'd never said it. It was just to make Stanners mad."

"Did it?"

"I'll say, I thought he was going to give me a bashing, but he didn't. My mum was a prostitute you know…"

"That's not what Aunty Vi told me. I heard that she was a nice girl who made a mistake and paid for it."

The discussion went on, and the complex web of lies and half-truths which had been fed to Phillip by members of his family – not, it appeared, by his adoptive parents but by assorted relatives – began to come clear. It was the beginning of the breakthrough for which staff had been waiting. Not yet me: I had too many memories of the battles we had waged in Byron House. But I could at least see that he was not all bad. I had no personal knowledge as to whether his bullying and racketeering in the house was continuing but in the club he was showing maturity and was playing an increasingly useful part in keeping things running smoothly without any suspicion of bullying or extortion.

We discussed Phillip at length in the privacy of our bedroom, and soon realised that we were both out of our depth. I had too many memories of past conflicts and Joyce, while desperately sorry for Phillip, was conscious of her inexperience in such uncharted waters and anxious not to upset things at his home.

We agreed again to put the problem to our psychologist for him to at least give us his advice, and preferably to take over the casework. But how to do it without betraying confidences?

In the event it was not too difficult. John was already an occasional and welcome visitor to the club and we simply arranged matters so that a visit coincided with Joyce being there. As had become quite usual, Phillip and Joyce were deep in a game of chess and John stood by watching. Joyce had to leave quite soon – at least that was the excuse – and John took over her game. We never did know exactly how the conversation developed, but somehow or other he got the whole story of Phillip's family and their references to his natural mother without betraying any of Joyce's confidences. I developed a new respect for the casework skill necessary for a psychologist.

Joyce was soon reassured that no harm had been done. On the contrary Phillip's feelings about his natural and adoptive mothers which had long been repressed needed to be explored. His contacts with Joyce, very near the same age as his natural mother, had stimulated his interests. It became clear that he had built up a romantic picture of his mother as an attractive, successful fairy queen sort of figure who, if only he could establish contact, would welcome him back into her life so that they could go forward into some sort of idyllic future. Could contact be arranged? At a case conference between school staff and social workers involved previously with Phillip and his adoptive family, it was agreed that we should explore possibilities. Of course nothing could go ahead without the prior and full approval of the adoptive parents, but the general view was that family relationships were in such a fragile and strained state that it was certainly worth exploring the possibilities.

Of crucial importance was the attitude of the natural mother. Her whereabouts were already known to her local children's department. She had married with a young family and it was most important that her family, by all account happy and settled, should not be put at risk. In the event it transpired that her husband was aware of all the circumstances, that she had previously made tentative enquiries about making contact and that there would be no difficulties raised on her part. Arrangements went ahead rapidly and a date for a visit was fixed. The initial contact was to be in the children's department office, with a home visit to follow if all went well. Transport was due to be provided by our social worker but there was a last minute hitch in these arrangements and I was drafted in. By a fortunate coincidence Joyce's parents were staying with us for a week so Joyce was able to make the trip with Phillip and me.

We set off with high hopes of a pleasant excursion. No responsibilities for organising the meeting – that was taken care of by the children's officer – and no need to be rushing back. In the event the journey was far from peaceful. Before we had gone twenty miles Phillip said he was feeling sick. We stopped by the roadside four times to allow him to stretch his legs. He was not sick and I felt he was just wasting time, so when he complained a fifth time I told him he must wait a while, we were already well behind schedule. He was promptly sick in the car! We stopped at the next petrol station to clean up as best we could but when we finally arrived at the children's office we were an hour late and Barbara, Phillip's mum, had had to go home to attend to her other children. All was not lost; she had agreed that Phillip could join the family for three hours or so to get to know everyone. It seemed a bit rushed to me but the arrangements had already been made and I could think of no valid objection. We were asked to follow a Child Care Officer in her car and were soon parked behind her in a rather run down council estate. No doubt it had been state of the art when it was built between the wars but it had not recovered from the years of neglect during the war. Number 36, where we were destined, was certainly no better that its neighbours.

We were quickly introduced, then our guide excused herself, saying she had to get back to the office. We could either go back to the office if time permitted after the visit or we could take Phillip straight back to school. "I expect you'll want to leave Phillip for a couple of hours with his mum. There's quite a nice café on the main road, just round the corner."

And what of Phillip? Pitchforked willy-nilly into his new family he looked totally ill at ease. His mother, far from being the beautiful sylph-like figure he had imagined, was a buxom, no-nonsense Lancashire lass. Certainly she made him welcome, rather too much so for his liking, for she enveloped him in what was meant to be a loving hug. "Come here and let me have a good look at you. By gum you're a strapping lad."

Phillip was squirming with embarrassment. We could almost see the cogwheels whirling in his brain: what have I let myself in for? No doubt he was making mental comparisons between the chaotic, untidy room in which we found ourselves and the orderly calm he was used to at home. His two half-brothers, eleven and ten years old, and their sister, perhaps eight, were playing a board game but at mother's insistence got up, rather reluctantly, to be introduced to the visitors. Mother bustled into the kitchen to make us a cup of tea, taking Phillip with her and leaving Joyce and me to chat to her other three. I was at a total loss as to how to make any sort of contact but Joyce soon put them at ease. In a very short time the little girl, Karen, was sitting beside Joyce on the settee showing off a painting book and the two boys had resumed their board game with me taking Karen's place.

Mum came back in with tea and cakes and invited us to stay for tea. We had a cup of tea and a generous slab of cake but politely declined anything further. "Phillip needs a bit of time to get to know you, so we'll leave you for a couple of hours before we have to set off back."

"That'll be good, Phillip, won't it?", said mum.

We were by no means sure that he agreed, but we left before he could raise any objection and went off to find the café we had been told about. We had a bite to eat, had another go at cleaning up the car at a convenient garage and sprayed it liberally with air freshener. It was soon time to pick up Phillip and we returned full of apprehension at what we would find. It was clear that things had not gone well in our absence. Barbara was doing her best, but for Phillip her best was simply not good enough.

We said our strained goodbyes, Joyce and I doing our best to pour oil on obviously troubled waters, and set off for the rather wearisome journey back to school. It was soon apparent that the trip was not to be full of fun, with car games to pass the time. Phillip was in a foul mood.

His meandering thoughts were passed on to us days later by John Briers who got him to write an account to 'get it out of his system'.

What do they think they're playing at trying to tell me that that thing is my real mum? My mum lives in London, she always has. When I was taken from her she went straight to London and now she's a model or an actress. She's beautiful not like that fat freak. She's not married – when she lost me she wasn't going to have any more kids.

It's not Mrs S. – she's decent, it's Stanners and Briers, they've cooked it up between them. If they think I'm having anything more to do with that fat cow they can think again. I'll stick with my Gloucestershire home and mum and dad. At least the place is clean and decent. And that tea – it was poison.

Stop the car, I'm feeling sick again! At least I'll get rid of their rotten food. I'd do it in the car but Stanners would make me clean it up this time. I'd run away but I'd rather be back at school...

John assured us that good would eventually come from the trip. At least Phillip, this essentially selfish and egocentric adolescent, would now have a more favourable view of his Gloucestershire base and of his parents, who at least offered him a decent home and a degree of love and security in a harsh world.

I was not surprised to hear that Phillip was blaming me for what he regarded as a total mess, but at least Joyce was still in his good books. We had a case conference to discuss further contact with real mum. It was unclear what steps, if any, we should take to disabuse Phillip of his fantasies of a glamorous model mother who lived in London and was just waiting to be reconciled with the son who had been snatched from her. The consensus, in the end, was that we could safely leave Phillip to his dreams; we were not at all certain that he believed them himself.

I had anticipated some problems at the first committee meeting after our return from Lancashire, but to my surprise Phillip seemed in benign mood and anxious to get on with normal business. Just as well, for we had a massive programme to organise. Visits to other clubs, participation in all the various boys' club competitions, weekend camps, canoeing trips and, most urgently, football coaching and team selection.

It was clear that I could not cover all the planned activities on my own. I presented Bill Hall and Dick Adams with a possible programme, indicating the approximate time requirements for each project, and had an urgent meeting with them to discuss how we would meet the staffing requirements. Bill Hall again offered help from other training school staff, pointing out that the popularity of the club was reducing demands on staff for other out of teaching hours activities. While appreciating the offer, a clear indication of progress after my dismal first six months, I declined with thanks. When the club was better established we could reconsider but for the time being I was quite firm that we did not want anything which would turn the club into just another school activity. At all costs we had to preserve our independence. I asked whether there were any funds available for some extra paid outside help – there weren't!

The only alternative I could offer was to prune the programme to fit in with the time I had available. I pointed out that I was already doing much more than the statutory requirement of fifteen hours a week extraneous duty for which I was paid. We went away to consider, but within a couple of days Dick Adams came up with a possible solution. Vic Wootten, the gardener instructor at the classifying school could, if I found him suitable, be transferred from extraneous duties at the classifying school to become assistant club leader at the training school.

Did I want him? Christmas had come early! I already knew Vic from occasional staff functions and thought he would be eminently suitable. Not a good disciplinarian but placid, easygoing and tolerant. Most importantly, when I interviewed him he was keen to have a go. I introduced him to the Boys' Committee and he was ready to start without delay.

With help in the club I could concentrate on getting the football team teams organised. I had minimal football coaching skills and if we were to make any sort of reasonable showing we needed outside help. We could, of course, get willing help from keen footballers on the school staff, but I had an instinctive feeling that we would end up being a school, not a club team. In the event Sam Chapman turned up trumps and recommended a friend, John Hill, a young man who was not only himself a keen footballer but wanted to gain some voluntary club experience before going on to do a full time training course. I invited him to come along to a club evening to test the waters and he seemed to fit in at once.

We had thirty-eight hopefuls turn out for the first practice session and picked two teams in time honoured fashion by selecting two captains to pick sides. With the inclusion of reserves, everyone interested was given a chance. John Hill was there to referee and give advice, while I ran the touchline and gave what encouragement I could. We had a general changeover at half time and then John and I compared notes. It became clear that we were going to be stretched to provide a senior team – for players seventeen and younger – but that we had excellent talent for the under-sixteens. The senior team would have to rely heavily on three talented youngsters who had already been approached by one of the local league clubs and signed up on their junior list.

Within days John had arranged follow-up coaching sessions and a practice match with a local team with which he was connected. I left team selection to him, all seemed to be going well and we awaited the first league match with keen anticipation. It was played at home, on a Wednesday evening with a good crowd of supporters from both teams. We won comfortably, and though we had been told that we were playing one of the weaker sides we were both encouraged and hopeful of the season to come.

Then the blow fell. Five of the most skilful players, including the three stars, decided that they did not need to attend a training session John had fixed up in the gym. We gave them a second chance, but they still did not turn up. Safe in the knowledge that the team could not do without them, they felt that their places in the team were assured. John and I agreed that no progress could be made with such indiscipline and to the astonishment of the five, and indeed of the rest of the group, when the team for the next match was announced on the club notice board none of the rebel five were included. We lost the next match by a wide margin but at least we established the principle that no one was indispensable and that good team discipline was essential for progress.

We looked forward with some optimism to a good season. If we could no longer anticipate a high finish in the league at least John and I thought the teams were in good heart. How wrong could we be? At the training session before the second match of the season we discovered widespread dissatisfaction about team selection.

"Why can't we accept Tinkler and Stanley in the team? They do their training every week with a professional coach, that's good enough surely?"

The arguments raged without being resolved. John, as coach, was adamant that he needed all the team to discuss tactics and practice together. He had my full support but we both realised that there were limits to our powers. Football, as in all youth clubs, was a voluntary activity and if boys declined to play for what was clearly going to be a struggling team there was little we could do about it. Three more of the team exercised their right not to play.

The senior team was already in tatters but a worse blow was to follow when we heard on the grapevine that two of our best remaining players were to be licensed within days and would therefore not be available to play. We had a crisis meeting of the Boys' Committee at which we did what we should have done earlier: we took a careful look at the players we had available and projected their availability for the rest of the football season. Since the better players were the older ones, who had been in the school longest, it was clear that on the basis of past experience half the team would be out of school before the season was over. They could not realistically be replaced with younger players, however keen, and we took an immediate decision that we must withdraw from the senior division and concentrate our resources on the under-sixteen league. I rang Tim Brightman and Sam Chapman with a heavy heart to give the news. It was little comfort to be told that we were not the only team to withdraw.

We could now concentrate on the younger players. The problem here was not shortage of players but of selecting from up to thirty keen aspirants. Some rotation of the team was possible but many would be disappointed. With Sam Chapman's help we were able to arrange some non-league, friendly matches with some other local clubs who were having similar problems. Even so, we were left with a small but vocal group of older players who could not be accommodated in any of our teams. Gerald, the former committee member from Wesley House, informed me quietly that Tinkler and Stanley, two of our reluctant senior stars, were in a foul mood and planning trouble. He had no idea what they were working up to and unfortunately I did not take the warning seriously.

The crisis came one evening when Joyce and I were having a night out and the club was left in charge of Vic Wootten. Most of the boys were on the playing field watching a football match between two local schools, and Vic was supervising a group in the swimming bath. In the absence of adult oversight a group of boys rampaged through the club premises, smashing the furniture and table tennis table, scrawling graffiti on the walls, and in general causing devastation.

Vic was waiting for us when we returned and we surveyed the melancholy scene together. We gave up counting the cost when we looked in the snooker room to find the cloth ripped beyond repair, two table legs smashed off, broken cues and missing snooker balls. Our tried and, up to then, successful ploy of assessing all damage in terms of the number of boys' subs needed to replace damaged items was not going to work. The timescale needed to accumulate sufficient funds in this way was far too great. Vic was devastated. I took him home for a consoling chat and a drink but I was not really much help for I was in black despair myself. As usual it was Joyce who set us on the way to recovery.

"It's not the end of the world, it's just money."

"Okay, but it's not just money, it's stuff we can't do without. We can't run a club without snooker and table tennis."

"How do you know? You haven't tried!"

There were some sources of encouragement. The Boys' Committee was called together for a crisis meeting and all the members were unanimous that the club must continue. Joyce was present by invitation, and offered practical advice as to how we might raise money – jumble sales, disco, sponsored swim, appeals to charities, car cleaning and so on. She fired us all with her own enthusiasm and common sense, and without more ado we set about putting things right. We closed the club for one evening only, and when we re-opened we had a rush of boys eager to see what it was like.

We had collected all the broken stuff together in one corner and we had an immediate meeting to discuss the future. Jeremy, a Wesley House boy whose parents were well off and kept him amply supplied with pocket money, suggested doubling weekly subscriptions until the damage was put right. This was shouted down. Desmond, a Carpenter House boy who never seemed to have any money, suggested that as there would now be so little to do in the club the subscriptions should be stopped. That suggestion too was vetoed. The most practical suggestions came from Phillip, who said he was sure that the broken tables could be repaired in the woodwork shop. And so it turned out – the shattered table tennis and snooker tables were repaired and reassembled in double quick time. The table tennis tables were as good as new, but we played snooker for months with a cloth whose rips were repaired with binding tape.

We collected heaps of jumble from neighbours. Among the rubbish they were glad to get rid of we had enough decent cast-offs and a few quite attractive individual items which, when we had our sale just two weeks later, we could set out on a speciality stall. We raised nearly £90, not a fortune but enough to pay for the worst damage and leave a balance enough to get new cloth for the snooker tables as soon as we could find a supplier. We were back in business, chastened by the thought of how close we had come to disaster, but encouraged by all the help and, above all, by the committee members, who were clearly thriving on their new responsibilities.

We never did find the culprits. The finger of suspicion pointed to our football rebels. Gerald, who had warned me of trouble to come, was unable to help further. I questioned as many of the members individually as I could manage but soon decided that the mystery was best left unsolved. Bill Hall made it clear that if we did find the perpetrators it was too serious a matter to be dealt with purely by club discipline. I could see and accept his reasoning, but still did not welcome the thought that we could not cope with it as a club. It was noticeable that none of the football rebels, the prime suspects, ever came into the club again. They were, in any case, all within two months of being licensed.

All the missing snooker balls, with the exception of one yellow, were eventually retrieved from various points of the grounds where they had been thrown. We replaced the yellow with a white-spot ball and though this caused some confusion when the wrong white was struck it was not a serious matter and certainly not worth the cost of replacing the whole set.

Vic Wootten was soon persuaded to stay on, with the heart-warming assurance from a large majority of members that he was welcome and well liked. Gerald, ever the club member to open his mouth and put his foot in it, expressed it perfectly.

"Don't go, Vic" – he was always Vic to the boys – "we like you better than Stanners."

Thank you Gerald!

Dick Adams and Bill Hall made light of my fears about the club's future. "If the club can survive this, as we believe it can, it could be all the better for having to face the challenges," was the encouraging verdict.

Although we had re-opened the club with only one day out of service it took a couple of weeks to clean up all the mess. Bill Hall offered help from the departments in working time. It was tempting but I felt that it would be much more effective as a learning experience if we dealt with it ourselves, in club time, and I declined the offer with thanks. I had my inner doubts, but in public expressed the view that not only would we survive but that, having faced all the challenges without outside help, we would in due course be all the stronger.

The single most encouraging development was the attitude of the Boys' Committee. To my astonishment, the prime mover in getting to grips with what needed doing was Phillip. With Raymond and the others he set about organising the clean-up with tremendous energy. Of course he had long experience in Byron House of getting others to do his work but on this occasion he worked as hard as, if not harder than, anyone else. Within just a few days the club rooms were spick and span: graffiti cleaned off or painted over, smashed windows repaired, rubbish disposed of, and all accomplished so far as I could see without any bullying or threats. Where was the Phillip who had caused me so much misery during my first six months? Discreet enquiries from staff indicated that there was no change in the house situation. I buttonholed Gary, my most reliable informant in Byron House, who, without my asking any direct questions, was more than willing to give me his opinions on the house, the club and life in general. What he said was not exactly calculated to boost my ego.

"I liked the house better when you were there, it was exciting, but it's more peaceful since you left."

"And what about Phillip?"

"What about him? He likes you and is very fond of Mrs S."

I felt a small glow of satisfaction but I should have finished the discussion at that point. When I expressed doubts, Gary readily agreed that he could have used the wrong word.

"I shouldn't have said 'likes'. He thinks you're better than some. Not bad."

And with that I had to be content, though I made a mental note that at some stage I should have some discussion with Phillip. Clearly our relationship was more comfortable than I had imagined.

Whatever the motivations, I could not fault the work being done under the leadership of the whole Boys' Committee and we were soon ready for a celebration evening. We invited the management committee, who just two weeks before had seen the devastation, to come and see the transformation. On the evening in question I was early in the club to ensure that everything was in order. I was in the committee room chatting to Phillip, who was, as always, smartly turned out. His tie was immaculately tied whereas mine, as I glanced in the mirror, was its usual shapeless mess. On a sudden impulse I asked Phillip how he managed always to have a tidy knot to his tie, as opposed to mine.

"It's the way you knot your tie, Sir. It's old fashioned. You should use a Windsor knot."

I confessed ignorance. "Would you show me how to do one?"

And so he did. I've been using Windsor knots in my tie from that day on. They are simple and effective and don't slip. Much more important to me was that this simple request for help marked a further definite thaw in our relationship. Not exactly brotherly love but certainly far from the bitter opposition of my Byron House days.

The evening went well. The visitors were suitably impressed and, having weathered the worst crisis of our short life, the club could go forward with confidence. To ease matters still further, the three boys whom we were certain were the main architects of the damage were licensed and left the school on the same day. None of the three came to me to say goodbye!

A couple of days after the school had said its official farewells to the three miscreants, half a dozen boys came, one after the other, to tell me the full story. There were apparently two others, besides the three now gone, who had been active participants. I saw the two boys in question and in due course they admitted their involvement. They were quite clearly not the ringleaders and after discussion with the Boys' Committee it was agreed that we would not take the matter any further. The boys had already voluntarily excluded themselves from the club; any further investigation would inevitably have meant that the whole miserable affair would be dragged up again. In all likelihood the three boys who had been the ringleaders would then have been recalled to the school under terms of their original Approved School Order. I could not see how this could benefit them or the school, and it would certainly not have been good for the club.

Maybe I was just rationalising a difficult situation, maybe it was just cowardice on my part, but whatever my motivations the decision stood and the three were left to pursue their careers. It was more than a year later that Peter Hanson, by then happily settled in a regular job and playing football for a local club as a semi-professional, visited the school and made a point of seeing me. He gave as near to an apology for the damage he had caused as was possible for a somewhat aggressive adolescent and thanked me for not interfering with his licence.

"You must have known who it was, we were dead scared afterwards. Thank you for not snitching on us. You're a decent bloke."

I let it pass without comment and wished him well for the future.

With the club refurbished and largely re-equipped we could plan ahead with increasing confidence. The football season was now well under way and the under-sixteens were doing creditably in the league. My Saturday afternoons were regularly taken up with matches around Bristol and I was frequently called on to referee. Not one of my strengths. Joyce and I had been keen spectators at the baseball ground in Derby in the halcyon days of the Rams, but I had no specialised training and did not possess even the most junior refereeing certificate. However, as a moderately useful cross-country runner I was at least fit and could keep up with the action. Equipped with a piercing official whistle and exuding a confidence I did not really feel, I got by. Of course in the 1950s and 1960s there was a much stronger tradition that the referee was right even when he was clearly wrong! Even so, at one rather memorable match in Bedminster Down I was heckled so strongly by a spectator who clearly supported our opponents that at half time I went over to him and offered him my whistle for the second half. He was a formidable looking character, but took my offer in good part, declined with thanks and moderated his criticism in the second half. His good humour was no doubt helped by the fact that I awarded his team a penalty when their centre forward was sent crashing to the ground by our centre half.

Encouraged by a spell of excellent late September weather we decided to organise a weekend camp. There was already a good stock of camping equipment in the school, which had not been used within the memory of the staff and was readily made available for club use. There were two large bell tents, a large, rectangular, ex-army heavy canvas tent, ideal as a dining and recreation area, and all the associated paraphernalia for cooking, washing, and so on. We rejected an antiquated three-seater toilet tent, the 'works' of which consisted simply of a polished board on stands with three appropriately cut holes. Presumably one had to dig latrine holes underneath, but since the site we were going to use was well appointed, rented by the local association of the NABC, we could leave the ancient relic behind. One of the older timers on the staff told me that the ancient loo had been a souvenir of the Zulu Wars of the 1870s, brought back by the son of a previous headmaster. The story was probably apocryphal but it made a good talking point for the boys.

Joyce and I were already seasoned campers and we were happy to take our two daughters, with our own up-to-date equipment. Joyce was happy to organise the supply side, and we were generously provided for by the school kitchen, with the full co-operation of the matron. We set off full of eager anticipation of a happy weekend in lovely surroundings. Vic Wootten was to come as the second member of staff and with just six boys we were well covered.

We had given the Boys' Committee first preference if they wished to come, as a reward for all the hard work they had put in to repair the damage to the club and get the place cleaned up. Four of the six accepted, and we ran a ballot to select the other two from the score or so of boys who expressed an interest. We loaded the Austin Welfarer with all our gear on Friday afternoon, Joyce checked the food stores and we set off for the short cross-country journey into the Somerset countryside. We negotiated with some difficulty the steep, narrow lane leading to the site and pitched up happily beside a crystal clear stream.

As a prudent measure Joyce drove our trusty Ford Popular with Kate and Christine. No seat belts or child seats in those days; Kate was used to car travel, and quite reliable, but Christine was too much of a live wire to be left unsecured. We devised a home made contraption from a child's chair to which Chris was secured by her child reins and which was in turn secured by luggage straps to the rear seat. Joyce followed the truck without difficulty and parked neatly beside it, somewhat pleased to be there safely as she had only recently passed her test.

Once the tents were up, we collected fallen branches from a nearby wood and soon had a campfire blazing happily away while the evening meal was cooking. Joyce had willing help from our own two girls and, surprisingly enough, from Phillip, and we soon enjoyed a splendid meal at outside tables lit by a Tilley lamp. The bushes by the stream were themselves lit up by hundreds of glow-worms, a sight never to be forgotten and the first time that Joyce and I had seen them. We had a happy sing-song including one which was a favourite of Kate's, much loved by her Brownie pack.

"Nobody loves me, everybody hates me. Think I'll go and eat worms. Bite their heads off, suck their juice up…" and so on. The boys loved it.

After a peaceful night and an early breakfast we were to set off for a long hike to the Cheddar Gorge. Vic Wootten was to go with the hikers, well set up with sandwiches for lunch, and either Joyce or I was going to take our two girls in the car while the other stayed behind with a volunteer boy to look after the camp, have a stroll in the countryside, and prepare the evening meal. I was quite willing to stay but knowing my lack of culinary skill Joyce insisted it should be her. She asked for someone to stay behind and help her and Phillip immediately jumped in to volunteer. In view of my past history with Phillip I should have perhaps put my foot down and insisted on someone else – there was no shortage of willing bodies – but Joyce indicated to me that she welcomed the opportunity to get to know him better. "… and anyway it will be good for the girls to have you on your own for the day."

The girls and I took a roundabout route to Cheddar, with a couple of hours by the sea at Weston on the way, and in due course met up with the hikers at our pre-arranged meeting point outside the Cheddar Caves. We had a picnic meal together and a tour around the main cave before it was time for the return journey. Gary, who by this stage had severely blistered feet, got a lift back in the car; the other four set off happily with Vic and made good time back to camp. Much to my surprise, we were greeted by Dick Adams, who had made an unscheduled and unexpected visit. While Phillip worked quite happily tidying up around the tents, and busying himself with preparations for the evening meal, Joyce had been quietly grilled about the school, her views on the club, and life in general, though I discovered this only later, as Dick stayed on to join us for our evening meal and a general chat with the boys.

It was an idyllic evening and just for once I felt totally relaxed in the presence of this complex and formidable character who had so put me through the mill at our first meeting in Derbyshire. What helped was that Joyce was clearly entirely happy in the company of her unexpected guest and even enlisted his aid to get our rudimentary dining furniture – simple folding tables and chairs – moved outside. The meal, a simple stew with vegetables followed by apple crumble and custard, passed happily. Kate sat between Phillip and Raymond on two extra cushions and I assisted Christine in her high chair. The atmosphere was happy and cheerful, and I could scarcely credit that it was these same boys, or some of them at least, who had given me such hell just a few months earlier.

The meal over and dusk descending, we hung Tilley lamps on convenient branches and cleared the decks for another sing-song. There was some argument as to who was to do the washing up. Joyce settled it by saying that she couldn't help because she had to get Christine ready for bed. We needed two willing volunteers. What was her particular magic? Somehow she managed to turn what would normally be an irritating chore to be dodged if possible into a desirable activity to be undertaken for the good of all. I did not know it at the time, but found out quite soon that it was Dick Adams's experience of Joyce on that day which finally settled our future career together. He was sure in his own mind that she, could, if she wanted it, have a career in child care. Although we neither of us appreciated it at the time, it was a truly momentous day.

When the boys were finally settled for the night and our two girls fast asleep, Joyce and I sat round the dying embers of the campfire and Joyce told me of her conversation with Phillip while they were working together. He had confided things to her which had plagued him for years and which, he recognised, had poisoned his relationships with his parents. Joyce, at that time, had no formal case work training, but she had an instinctive empathy with this troubled boy which had clearly got through to him and which led him to confide in her. What immediately worried me was that it was clear that she was more emotionally involved with Phillip than she should have been if she was to take a balanced view of his overall needs.

"I'm sure you're right," said Joyce with commendable tact when I put this to her, "but Phillip's hurting so much, doesn't know what to do about it, and doesn't want to go home when his licence comes up next month or the month after."

I could feel the sorrow in Joyce's voice and thought I saw tears in her eyes as she gave me the whole sad story. I asked her if she had Phillip's permission to tell me. She was indignant. "Of course I asked Phillip. You don't pass on private conversations as painful as that without permission. Phillip wants you to know because he thinks you can help, but doesn't want to tell you himself."

So much for all the social work short courses I'd attended in order to hone my casework skills. Joyce worked on instinct, with natural inbuilt skill and an emotional involvement with her 'client' (a hateful word which she would never have recognised: her 'clients' were children with hopes and dreams who needed love). With that approach, simple to state but difficult to practise, she could break through the armour of indifference, antagonism and suspicion to find the vulnerable individual underneath. It had served her well with Phillip: in the few short weeks she had got to know him and a few hours working with him on the mundane tasks of getting a meal ready she had broken through as no one to my knowledge had done before.

The story she told in graphic terms was of a middle-class home where everything on the surface appeared fine. Respectable members of the community, his father a successful and prosperous businessman, no shortage of material goods, toys, clothes or expensive holidays, but according to Phillip no real love between the parents or for him.

"They only adopted me because it looked good to the neighbours and friends, they never really wanted me."

Phillip's parents didn't row publicly: that would have let them down with the neighbours. There was no violence: that would be infra dig. Indeed, theirs was a home which, if not entirely brimming with excitement and *joie de vivre*, was at least, so far as the neighbours, the mother's bridge club, her church and the father's golf club were concerned, the epitome of middle-class respectability. Phillip's story was not of bitter rows but of scant evidence of love. No happy outings. Holidays which had to be endured rather than enjoyed. Days and weeks of silence. No beatings, no harsh words, but a total absence of affection.

"I'd rather he did lose his temper and give me a good hiding occasionally. At least it would show he cared. I can't understand why they don't get divorced. They don't sleep in the same bed any more…"

The catalogue of unhappiness went on and the anguish came through even though the information was at second hand.

"So what does Phillip want us to do?"

"He just doesn't know. As things are now he simply doesn't want to go home, but he doesn't have any alternative to suggest. In any case we only have Phillip's side of the story, we don't know what the parents think."

I cautioned Joyce about placing too much reliance on what Phillip said, but she was convinced she had the truth of the situation. Thinking back to the only time I had met the parents I believed she was right. Why had I not seen it for myself? How was it that Joyce, with no formal training, had got so close to this troubled adolescent so quickly when I, experienced and trained, had failed so dismally for so long. Was there even a twinge of jealousy on my part? Perhaps there was but I was also proud of the breakthrough she had achieved so quickly.

We talked on until the fire was just a few glowing embers and then went to bed. I gave Joyce a hug as we settled down and to my surprise her cheeks were wet with tears.

"What's the matter, sweetheart?"

"Nothing really. I'm sad for Phillip and his family but happy that we have each other and our two daughters."

"And what about Dick Adams? How long was he here? What did he want?"

"He was here for nearly two hours before you came back and we talked about all sorts. He did ask about Phillip – wanted to know whether this was the same boy who'd been so difficult with you, wasn't I at all afraid of him? I assured him that I wasn't, that Phillip was in fact being most helpful, and had volunteered to stay behind with me."

"What else did you talk about?"

"Well, I could see he wanted some private conversation so I sent Phillip off to get some wood for the camp fire and then he asked me whether I wanted to work in the school. I told him that I was already helping in the club. He said he knew that already but that he meant paid work."

Joyce had told him it was not possible while Christine needed her at home, but it was clear she found the idea intriguing. Despite her disclaimer I could see that a seed had been sown, and that it had fallen on fertile ground.

CHAPTER 5

Ambitions

When we returned from camp I should by all reasonable indications have been content with life. The club was spick and span, well attended and flourishing. The classroom work was going smoothly, even with the department boys on Wednesdays. Joyce was clearly on top of the world after her conversation with Dick Adams and could see the possibility of a new and exciting career. Kate was happily settled in an excellent infant and junior school and we were all increasingly settled in the community. I had joined a local bridge club and Joyce had accepted the secretaryship of a newly formed ladies' group in the church, an evening group to complement the existing ladies' meeting which met in the afternoons and was therefore inaccessible to working mums. We had regular excursions to Bristol theatres and a reliable babysitter. What more could we wish for?

And yet I was increasingly restless and discontented. My experience in Byron House still rankled and in my twisted thinking could only be exorcised if I could put the house situation right. That could only come about if I was appointed to a senior position. I got on well now with Dick Adams and Bill Hall, and they might possibly accept me as deputy head, but it was the managers and the Home Office Inspectorate who had to ratify senior appointments. My disastrous experiences in Byron House were well known to all and cast long shadows over my career: if

I was to have a senior position I would have to look elsewhere than Kingswood.

I confided my fears to Joyce and she was, to say the least, not pleased.

"Your future, and mine are here. Stick it out and have a go for the deputy's job which is coming up soon. And I want to have a go at the assistant matron's job."

"So that's it, you've got it all mapped out. You start work, I make a fool of myself applying for a job they won't give me and we go on as we are."

Even as I said it I knew I was being grossly unfair. Joyce was eminently suitable for the job which could be hers, and essentially I was being a selfish chauvinist pig. I didn't admit this at the time; instead I dropped a bombshell.

"There's a job in the *Times Ed* which interests me, a deputy headship at an approved school in Cambridgeshire. It's ten miles from Ely and sounds good."

We had an increasingly acrimonious argument on and off throughout an evening after the children had gone to bed. Kate came down at one stage to see what I was shouting about. That shocked me somewhat and we both broke off to comfort her. We resumed more quietly but no less bitterly when Kate was safely off to sleep with a goodnight kiss from both of us.

Even as I was arguing I knew in my heart that what Joyce was saying was sensible. I should at least apply for the deputy's job here.

"You may get it," said Joyce. "I believe you stand a good chance, but even if you don't we shall both be working together. I would like the assistant matron's job – there I said it and I believe I can do it well."

My bitterness came through. "So I tag along on your coat tails…"

"Oh for heavens sake grow up. I thought you were happy here. We came to Kingswood because you were bored at Alfreton didn't we? Do we move now because you're bored?"

"We did not come here because I was bored, we came because—"

At that precise moment Kate came down again.

"I can't get to sleep, mummy."

By the time she was comforted and back to bed, my moment of crisis had passed.

"Because what? Why did we come to Kingswood?"

Had I really been going to say that we came because Joyce had seen the advertisement and pushed me into applying? I hope not; it would have been quite despicable to put the responsibility on Joyce. I don't think I would have been so destructive, but I was glad of the further opportunity to think more carefully.

"We came because we both wanted to and in spite of all that happened in the first few months we've been happy."

"Well then, why move? Give me one good reason."

"Well it would be handy for the Norfolk Broads, and we've always wanted to go sailing."

"That's a pathetic reason. We could easily have some sailing in Gloucestershire."

There was no way we could resolve the argument sensibly. In the end Joyce said that I could please myself but she was going to bed. "Go and talk it over with Bill Hall or Dick Adams, preferably both. If you don't I will."

She knew which buttons to press. I could not again have her speaking on my behalf. I would see them myself.

Not surprisingly Dick Adams had a good knowledge of the school in question. As preparation for running a classifying school he had visited a considerable number of schools in each region, essential in making the decision about which school was best for a particular boy. He told me that the school was small but well thought of in the area, and that if I wanted to apply for the deputy's job he would not stand in my way.

"I expect you'll be called for an interview and even if you decide you don't want the job it will be good experience."

In due course I applied and was called for interview. Wives were invited to see the living accommodation, so Joyce's mum came down to look after the children for a couple of days and we duly set off for Cambridgeshire. The school was about ten miles from Ely, way out in the country. Three men, one single and two with wives, were shown around the school. After conversations with the head, his deputy and such staff as were not fully taken up with the boys, we were transported to a pub in the village where an evening meal and bed and breakfast had been booked for us. Formal interviews were to begin at 9.30 the following morning.

The head began by giving the five of us a brief history of the school and then asked if the wives would mind staying in the staff room while he saw each of the men in turn. We would also see his deputy to find out from him about duty rotas and the like. It was a pleasant, informal procedure which, so far as I was concerned, went quite well until I started talking to the deputy head. He was a pleasant, affable man in his mid-fifties who soon explained that he was taking early retirement, which he much regretted, on grounds of ill health. He had been at the school for seventeen years and had seen it through the war years, for two of which he had been acting head. He was obviously totally bound up in every aspect of school life, but it was when I asked about duties and duty rotas that alarm bells began to ring for me.

"Oh, we don't have duty rotas as such. I'm here most of the time and live in the main school block so I'm happy to cover.

It's not a problem. The head will stop in whenever I want a day off."

Not a problem for him, but it certainly would be for me! When the three of us went back to the head for a further joint session before we went off for the night he eulogised his present deputy as one in a thousand and it was pretty clear he was looking for someone in the same mould. It would certainly not be me, and I was interested to note that the other married candidate felt exactly the same. Both of us were quite prepared to give the only single candidate a clear run if, indeed, he wanted the job. I told Joyce the outcome of my thinking. She was not surprised: she had already come to the same conclusion herself. The only question was whether to stay for the interview or not. In the event we did stay but all three of the candidates asked such pointed questions about duties and responsibilities that we were all deemed unsuitable. In due time the post was re-advertised but whether they would ever find such a paragon as the present deputy was, to say the least, doubtful.

We returned to Kingswood not at all dismayed. We had had an enjoyable three days and came back to what had become a familiar lifestyle with renewed vigour and enthusiasm. I saw Dick Adams and gave him an edited account of the proceedings. His comment was that the place had not changed and that he was not at all surprised that I was not interested. "A good experience which will help you to feel more settled," was his summing up.

Joyce, delighted to be back home and looking forward herself to a new career, made no capital at all out of the fact that she had been right and I had been wrong about the Cambridgeshire job. Instead she concentrated her energies on getting me to apply for the deputy head's job. The advertisement had already been published and the closing date for application was just a week away, with interviews to be held ten days later. This was to be quite separate from the assistant matron's job, which was to be settled later. In spite of Joyce's enthusiasm and her confidence in me I was, to say the least, hesitant.

Certainly the club was now well established and the classroom work was running smoothly, but the memories of my first few months in Byron House were still fresh and raw, and the scars ran deep. I was happy with running the club and not at all sure that I could cope with the added responsibility. I got on well with all the staff but they had all seen the difficulties I had endured and moreover I was the youngest member. Would friendships survive a change of responsibility? Was it worth taking the risk? In any case, as I said to Joyce when she continued to press me, "They certainly won't give me the job with my record."

"Well in that case you've nothing to lose except your pride, have you? Go for it."

Without committing myself I collected an application form and job details from the office and waited somewhat apprehensively for reactions from staff. It was a certainty that news of my interest in the job would soon be common knowledge. My bridge partner wished me well and my badminton partner said, "Better you than me," and that's as far as it went. I didn't know whether to be miffed or pleased, but at least I could detect no change in the attitude of my friends. However, three days before applications were due in I still had not made up my mind and Joyce lost patience.

"I've cleared the dining room table, Kate's at school and I've arranged for Christine to be looked after by Mrs Jepson. Let's get it sorted."

This we did, after further mumblings from me about not really wanting the job. Quite untrue: I knew in my heart I would love the position; my doubt was whether I could do it. When I thought back over my life to date I was only too well aware of other mishaps and catastrophes along life's road which had had profound effects on my development. Full of apprehensions but buoyed up by Joyce's faith in me I set about producing a curriculum vitae. Although not formally necessary for the application, I felt it would be useful to review my life, and in particular those catastrophic events which had proved so formative. I did not want to repeat past errors of judgement, or to make new ones.

. . . . .

I had a happy childhood as the eldest of six children, though life was often a struggle. Dad was a coal miner but found himself out of work after the general strike in 1926, and we were very poor. In 1930 Mam collapsed in the street from malnutrition and suffered the indignity, as she saw it, of being taken to the clinic to be given protein-rich drinks. That was the signal for a family fight back. Dad took on a second allotment garden and I and my brothers were roped in to help. The nearest water supply was half a mile away and one of our main tasks was to carry water in any period of low rainfall. In the end Dad used his mining skills to dig a deep well, which he lined with bricks scavenged from where old houses were being demolished. With two productive gardens, including a few chickens, we were never again short of food and, indeed, had some to spare to sell to those few neighbours who had a little more money than us.

These circumstances perhaps had little reference to my possible application though they certainly shaped my attitude to life. What was undoubtedly relevant was the education I received. This began at home. Dad was intelligent and well read and, in spite of our poverty, we had a considerable collection of books, mainly Odhams classics including a complete set of Dickens. I read voraciously from an early age, something I much preferred to the street games so popular with my contemporaries. My formal education began in a C of E infant school a mile and a half from where we were lodging at the time. I was collected each morning by Miss Radford, a teacher who lived nearby and who walked three or four of us to school each morning.

When I was five we moved to a newly built council house, with the luxury of a bathroom and hot water on tap, and I changed to another C of E infant's school. This was where I met the lady who, apart from my parents and my mother's sister who lived with us throughout my boyhood, was to be the major influence in my life – Miss Purchase, the headmistress. She encouraged my reading, was kindly but strict and followed my progress not just through her school, which was for less than two years anyway, but also throughout my educational years and beyond. Without her influence I would certainly not have been a teacher and would not in any circumstances have been contemplating a deputy headship.

The crunch came with the eleven-plus. It was fiercely competitive in those days and the all-age school I had trans-ferred to by then seldom had any scholarship winners. In any case it did not apply to me because I was quite seriously ill for two months before the examination and not able to sit it. Logically it should have been the end of all my grammar school ambitions but Miss Purchase stormed the citadel of Shire Hall on my behalf and I was given special dispensation, along with a couple of others, for a resit. I duly passed but was not yet out of the wood for there was no way my parents could afford the necessary school uniform. Of course I could have gone in whatever clothes I had but I would have stuck out like a sore thumb; for a sensitive soul such as I was it would have been purgatory. Again it was Miss Purchase who stepped in to help, buying the uniform and all the necessary oddments to start me off. I remember shedding a few tears when I showed her the letter confirming my entry to the school. She told me not to be silly but I think there were tears in her eyes too. She was one of a whole generation of First World War spinsters whose fiancées had been killed and I, plus one or two others, were the children she never had. "Just do well at school and make sure you show me your reports."

I was immensely proud when I showed her my first report and was top of the form. I was not even disappointed when she picked on some subjects where there was some criticism. "Well done – but you will need to work harder at Physics and Latin."

I did well throughout my years at the grammar school and Miss Purchase thought that I should take a senior scholarship and go to Oxford or Cambridge. The school persuaded my parents that, even with all the grants which might be available, Oxbridge would be too expensive and I settled for teacher training at Borough Road in London, where I hoped to take a degree. Not possible in the event – the second war was upon us.

I attempted to join the University Air Squadron, which would have given me exemption while I trained for flying duties, but failed the medical on the eyesight test despite having attempted to cheat by learning the chart off by heart. In all probability this particular failure was a life saver, as the average life expectancy for young flying crew was short. In the event I was called up after a year in college in October 1942, a few days after my nineteenth birthday.

Due primarily to my incompetence in military matters, I did more training in the army than most ex-soldiers I have spoken to. Six weeks initial training in Norwich; sixteen weeks with the Sherwood Foresters in Lincoln training as an infantry signaller;

eight weeks in Pre-OCTU in Kent (it should have been six but was extended by two weeks of compassionate leave when my father was killed in a works accident); twenty or more weeks at Royal Signals OCTU in Catterick, including the disastrous battle camp experience detailed elsewhere; returning to Lincoln and the Sherwood Foresters for eight weeks; six weeks with 35 Division in Morpeth to give me a chance to redeem myself as an officer; before finally they decided that my talents could be put to some use and I completed a twenty-week training course as a radio mechanic. At this point I should, by rights, have gone abroad – Burma or Egypt perhaps – but fortunately someone discovered that I spoke reasonable French and from then on I had the job of shepherding units of Free French troops through the course in which I had just qualified. That took me through to the end of the war, by which time I had achieved the exalted rank of Lance Corporal.

Once hostilities ceased, life in our signals unit became humdrum, rather boring. One thing that occupied us was the smashing up of very large quantities of equipment which were surplus to army requirements. When we asked the reason we were told that if, for instance, huge quantities of radio valves were released onto the home market it would kill off what was then a flourishing British industry.

My army career finished in March 1946 when I was demobbed, complete with an ill fitting, two-piece demob suit and a not very generous resettlement allowance. I immediately applied for, and was appointed to, a temporary teaching post at a local infant school – unqualified and poorly paid but very useful experience. I started off teaching a mixed class but after just a couple of days it was realised that I could not cope with the seemingly endless handicraft lessons. Instead, all the boys in this small school were separated out and I took charge of them in my own classroom for a term and a half. The only concept of infant teaching I had went back to my own infant school days. Much ritual chanting of phonics to teach reading, multiplication tables as an introduction to arithmetic, and much copying of exercises from the blackboard. Instead of handicraft we had PE and games on the nearby recreation ground and all in all we had a smashing time. I had a column of youngsters, not just boys, who trailed me to school each day, and I think we all enjoyed the experience.

Less enjoyable was the experience of returning to college to complete my teaching certificate. Those two terms were a farce for all concerned, as everyone who had been called up during their training from 1939 to 1945 returned to college together. There were no extra staff or facilities, and the system was simply overwhelmed: lectures were crowded, there were no real checks as to whether students attended or not and any written work produced was, to say the least, perfunctory. The college rules, which had seemed reasonable when we were first there, now seemed petty and bureaucratic to men some of whom had witnessed unimaginable horrors. We had parachutist survivors of Arnhem, ex-prisoners of war and some who had seen the horrors of the concentration camps with their gas chambers. It is no doubt unfair to criticise college staff, who were working under great difficulties and did their best to fit us in to a system creaking at the seams. I'm sure they were happy to see the back of us after two terms and, after some rather derisory assessment process, we were all passed out with average grades.

My own grade was, I imagine, the lowest possible without actually failing, due to the sort of accidental circumstances that seemed to litter my career. Each of us had to be seen once by an HMI while on teaching practice. By a malevolent fate my final teaching practice was in a large secondary school in Acton and up to the very last day I had not been seen by anyone from the college, the school or the inspectorate. I was congratulating myself on having got away with it, for I had a horribly unruly lower stream mixed class whose thoughts were certainly on the coming holiday and not on work. It was the thirteenth of December 1946 and I was to be married in Derbyshire at 11am on the fourteenth. Was it Friday the thirteenth? It was certainly unlucky for me, for at the first lesson in the afternoon an inspector walked in and introduced himself.

"Do carry on, Mr Stanway, as though I was not here."

Carry on with what? Could I do what I had planned and read them a story? Not really: the timetable said 'Mathematics' and that's what I was supposed to be doing. I contemplated telling the inspector that I was to be married the next day and throwing myself on his mercy but I chickened out and ploughed on with some algebraic equations which I had been asked to deal with and which proved quite incomprehensible to the class.

In the circumstances the inspector's comment that I seemed out of my depth, and that my preparation had been inadequate, was entirely fair. When he asked what the two large cases were doing at the back of the room, I told him that I was due to catch a train from Kings Cross to Nottingham and that I was to be married the next day. He unbent slightly, wished me well and said he quite understood why I was distracted. He did not, however, lift my grade and it was fortunate for me that my first headmaster made a point of not reading college reports, preferring to judge for himself. Not that that made much difference in my case – I have already detailed the disasters of my first two terms at Alfreton, never quite obliterated by the successful and happy years that followed.

I had one further disastrous episode to take into account for my curriculum vitae. In my third year of teaching, after my successful relegation year with 1R, I decided, quite impulsively, to complete my studies with an external degree. What I should have done was to have a year off, with fees covered by the state for ex-servicemen, in order to take the examination in a leisurely fashion. But never having had any difficulty with exams I decided on a different route and planned to do it all in my spare time. Unfortunately I had the wrong mix of subjects at Higher School Certificate level so to take the arts degree I wanted I had to add Latin to my portfolio. No difficulty, I thought, I had studied it without problems to the fifth form. A bit of revision, a look at a few past papers and I would be home and dry. I duly entered and in due course sat the examination in Nottingham. It was humiliating. In the ten years since I had done Latin at school the rust had eaten through and I was totally lost. I left the exam halfway through and made my miserable way home. I never did take Latin again and it was only years later that I took a sabbatical year to complete a degree course.

. . . . .

I discussed all this with Joyce and shared with her my anxiety that applying for the deputy's job could be another disaster.

"You'll never know if you don't try, will you? And what if we get someone we just can't get on with, what then?"

I gave way. In the end I did not even put together a curriculum vitae but submitted a simple covering letter with the formal application, saying that I was very happy in the school, that whatever the outcome of the interviews I hoped that the youth club would continue, and that perhaps its principles of self government could usefully be applied to some other areas of school life. So far as the schoolroom and departments were concerned a revision of curricula was needed to come more into line with modern practice; a good deal of staff discussion would be in order. I made no reference at all to my difficulties in Byron House. They were well known anyway, and there was no value in labouring the point – the house parents were leaving in less than a month having attained the post in a small children's home they had been looking for. Even more importantly Phillip was rapidly coming up towards licence. These circumstances would make it an ideal time for change and for establishing a new regime.

A serious drawback to the job for me was the disciplinary aspect, and in particular the occasional use of corporal punishment. Only the head and the deputy were allowed to administer this. The conditions were strictly laid down. It was to be on the bottom, through the usual trousers, and the number of strokes, never more than six but seldom more than two or three, was to be properly recorded in a punishment book and in due time reported to the managers. The cane was used mainly for persistent absconders and for vicious bullying. In the circumstances of the time it was certainly acceptable and though the disciplinary framework of the school did not depend on the cane one could not deny that the knowledge of this ultimate sanction was a help to keeping good order. The difference between good order and good discipline was a philosophical distinction which was due to be looked at shortly, as we were to have a good look at a new rewards and privileges scheme.

In my pre-occupation with the deputy's job – whether I was up to it, whether I should apply and worries about the possible humiliation of an interview – I had temporarily forgotten Joyce's conversation with Dick Adams and his suggestion that she might take up a paid position. She said that she would like to have further conversation with Adams and with Florence Collinson, the matron, to find out how possible it was to fit the duties round her family responsibilities. This was a first essential if she was to take the job.

"Wait a minute," I said, "what do you mean 'if you take the job'. You don't know whether you would get it."

"Oh, I think so, that's certainly what Dick Adams meant. The job's not to be advertised and there's no one else on the staff that's up for it."

I had a sudden flare-up of jealousy. Was this what it was all leading up to? Was my position secondary to the appointment of Joyce? As usual Joyce was ahead of me, reading me like a book.

"You're jealous, aren't you?"

"Of course I'm not."

"Well, that's all right then, I'll tell Dick Adams and Florence that I'll take the job providing I can sort things out for the family. It shouldn't be difficult. Kate's at school and when the boys are in classes or departments I can take Christine around with me. She'll love it and on the odd occasions that's not possible Mrs Jepson will come in. She'll welcome the money.

"You've got it all worked out, haven't you? Is it any use my saying anything?"

Even as I said it I realised how mean-spirited it was. The prospect of working together was the fulfilment of a dream. I was simply grumpy that I wasn't calling the shots. I took back, as far as I possibly could, all my jealous thoughts and told her to go ahead. When I thought about it further it was obvious that she was excited about the whole idea and that she would be going ahead anyway. It was far better and certainly easier, for me to go with the flow. In due course Joyce saw the principal and the matron and came back with pretty much a free hand to organise the necessary work in any way which suited. Her appointment was assured, and would be ratified at the next meeting of the managers without even a formal interview.

One arm of our dream working partnership was apparently secure. It just remained for me to have a successful interview, assuming, of course, that I would be called – by no means certain, in view of the various disasters that had sprinkled my career so far. I was interested to find that there were no other internal candidates. There would certainly be considerable interest in the post from other approved school staff. Kingswood, with its classifying school, was at the centre of work with delinquent youth in the region that covered the whole of the Southwest and beyond stretching from Birmingham to Land's End. Dick Adams was well known in all the schools in the region and indeed nationally.

In a very short time, interviews were arranged and I was invited along with three other candidates – two already working in approved schools and one from a grammar school. Interviews were to take place over two days. The first day we were addressed by Bill Hall, who filled us in on the school background, arranged a tour of the premises, and confirmed the details of the formal interviews to be held the following day. Overnight accommodation for the visitors had been arranged in the classifying school and we were all to join resident staff there for an evening meal. The grammar school master, after a private interview with Bill Hall, told us that after due thought, although he liked the idea of working with delinquents, he preferred to stay with his present job as a head of science and would be withdrawing his candidature. He lived not too far away and did not stay to the evening meal. The three of us who were left had an interesting evening chatting in general terms and no doubt weighing each other up as potential rivals. I got on well with both of them, both older than me and certainly both with longer experience of work in the field. I decided that whichever one was appointed, I could work happily with him and went home to tell Joyce that I was resigned to carrying on as club leader, at least for some years to come. As ever, her response was to the point. "Don't be a defeatist, or you won't get the job – just go for it."

And so to the formal interviews. The usually impeccable intelligence service had let me down, and I had no prior knowledge of who our inquisitors were to be. Dick Adams and Bill Hall obviously, with a Home Officer inspector to add gravitas, and I was told that there would no doubt be three of the managers. We were asked to wait in Bill Hall's office until we were called for interview, comfortably seated with coffee and biscuits for refreshment. Half an hour before interviews were due to start I had a temporary lift when two managers I knew well arrived together and were escorted into the main committee room. Miss Keen had confirmed my original appointment and I had got to know Mr Biscoe reasonably well as he had taken quite an interest in the boy's club.

My frisson of hope was short lived. A minute later a taxi drew up and the imposing figure of Brigadier Johnson alighted to be conducted in by the school secretary. It was the good Brigadier whom I had firmly put in his place in my classroom just a few months before. At the time I had no idea that the Brigadier had in fact taken no offence at my rudeness, but paradoxically his arrival, and the certainty that his presence scuppered my chances, stiffened my resolve. With, as I saw it, nothing to lose I determined to give no quarter and to go down fighting.

The interviews were conducted in alphabetical order, so with Stanway being near the end of the alphabet I had plenty of time to consider my options. None of them looked good. My fellow candidates, with whom I had become quite friendly over the past twenty-four hours, came out of the committee room to join me in the head's office looking relieved to have got it over but both saying they felt they had had fair interviews. When Bill Hall came to summon me for my ordeal I was relatively calm. By now quite convinced that the job was not to be mine, I was simply determined to put up as a good a performance as possible. The Brigadier was acting chairman for the afternoon.

"Sit down, Mr Stanway, would you like a cup of tea?"

Not likely, I'd probably spill it down my shirt! "No, thank you Sir, we've been well catered for while we've been waiting."

Squinting over the top of his glasses the Brigadier pitched a body blow.

"If I remember correctly we met in your classroom, nine days after you arrived here, did we not?"

Any lingering hopes that the incident was forgotten, or that it was not on his mind disappeared. Not only did he remember the incident, he could recall the exact time.

"If I remember correctly you put me very firmly in my place, did you not?"

What could I say? An apology would have been pointless and would certainly have cut no ice with this man, whose excellent war record I had looked up for myself out of curiosity. I was searching for some innocuous and vapid comment when to my astonishment he cut me short.

"I was out of order – you were quite right. My apologies."

Could this be right? An apology? When I looked at him, he had quite a twinkle in his eyes. I had a flicker of hope that all was not quite lost.

A few general questions from the managers and the questioning was then turned over to Bill Hall and Dick Adams. I was doing reasonably, I thought, until the issue of the boys' club was brought up by Dick Adams. It started innocently enough with congratulatory comments on the way the club had developed and had overcome some major setbacks. We explored together, for the benefit of the managers, the philosophy of the club and, in particular, its ability to run almost entirely independently of school discipline. I agreed with Bill Hall that this freedom could not include dealing with absconding or stealing out of school. He agreed that we had established a system which coped with these requirements without abandoning the principles on which the club was founded. It was then that Dick Adams fired a blockbuster.

"We can agree that the club is doing very well, and we all like it. We wouldn't want to lose it. Can you let us know how, if you are appointed deputy head, you will combine it with being club leader."

This was a question I had already examined for myself. I knew what the answer should be. There was no possibility that I could combine the roles of club leader and deputy head. It was a battle we had fought and won when the club was established – that Dick Adams, Bill Hall and his deputy would be welcome guests in the club from time to time but only by invitation. No way could a deputy head, with his responsibilities for school discipline, be a regular in the club as leader. The issue could not be shirked and there could be no misunderstanding.

"I could not be both deputy head, and club leader. The two posts are simply not compatible."

The follow-up punch came from Bill Hall. "Which, then, is more important to you – being club leader or being deputy head?"

"Well naturally being deputy head, or I wouldn't have applied."

The interview meandered on. Some general questions about the family. Dick Adams said it was hoped that, whatever happened with the deputy's job, Mrs Stanway would be working in the school. Miss Keen asked how the children had settled. Mr Biscoe questioned me on my Methodist background and what I thought about compulsory church attendance for the boys.

Finally I was asked whether I wanted to ask any questions or make any comments. I had no questions – I was already fully familiar with school policy and what would be expected of the deputy in terms of duties – but if I was to stand any chance of getting the job which I now, somewhat to my surprise, desperately wanted I had to clarify the panel's thoughts about the club. I went into some detail about the club philosophy as I saw it, to make it clear that the disciplinary role of deputy head, integral and essential to the job, would preclude combining the job with club leader. If appointed I would support the club in other ways, using my contacts in church and community, but would leave leadership to Vic Wootten. I would also look to apply some of the principles of self-government that worked so well in the club into the general school framework, and in particular into the house structure. This was Bill Hall's cue to ask me one final question – the most awkward reserved till last – about my record in Byron House.

"You know, as I do, that you had considerable disciplinary problems in the house. How will that affect your work as deputy head?"

"As deputy head, not at all. I would hope to be able to assist the newly appointed housemaster in whatever way necessary. There will be changes anyway."

I was told to join the others, that a decision would be made shortly, and that we would be informed at once. In due course Bill Hall came to the office, thanked the three of us for our attendance, assured us that we had all been excellent candidates and announced that the post of deputy head was to be offered to Mr Stanway. I lingered for a while to wish my fellow candidates well for the future and went home on cloud nine to give Joyce the news. Such was the efficiency of the Kingswood rumour mills that she had already been told!

Although my appointment would not start officially until the end of the month, some three weeks away, there was no time to sit back and relax. Bill Hall, who had already had nearly two months of full-time overall responsibility for the school, was ready for a break and I was equally keen to start work. It did occur to me that if either of the other candidates had been appointed Bill Hall would have had another two months' wait and his forthcoming holiday, already twice deferred, would be put back yet again. How much had that consideration affected his choice? I would never really know, but whatever the full circumstances of my appointment I was delighted.

And Joyce? Having finally pushed me into applying, she was over the moon. This was, in her view, another step along the career path she had seen for me when she had spotted the advert eighteen months before. The fact that she was now to have a new career of her own was an unexpected but delightful bonus.

CHAPTER 6

Working together

"We won't let you down, Sir, on Saturday. We'll bash hell out of the Eastville lot. We've got weapons."

"What do you mean, weapons?"

"We been making them ready for the fight."

"What fight?"

"On Saturday in the cinema car park. They've challenged us but we'll smash 'em to bits."

This surreal conversation was between me, newly installed as deputy head in full charge of the school, and Desmond, a gangling sixteen-year-old from Carpenter House and far too naïve to be inventing such an unlikely story.

"I'll show you, Sir."

He took me round to the garden shed at the back of the school and showed me with some pride a cache of weapons – assorted clubs, sharpened blades, a couple of flick knives, and some large bolts whose use I could only guess at. I was three and a half weeks into my new post, and disaster was already looming.

· · · · ·

It was only four weeks before my conversation with Desmond that I had been appointed deputy head. Bemused and bewildered by the successful outcome of what I had expected to be a disastrous interview, I had set about preparing for my responsibilities with considerable energy. I re-read the Approved School Rules, chatted to all the staff individually and as house groups, and struggled to familiarise myself with all the different syllabuses and records of work done.

I was in a frenzy of activity as I only had a very short time before Bill Hall was going off for three weeks for a long overdue holiday. We were, in due course, to have an official appointment of a third-in-charge. This was to be an additional teacher or instructor who would, in addition to a full teaching timetable, share overall responsibility for the school. However, the appointment would not be made until the Home Office approved the entire funding necessary. In the meantime it was Bill Hall or myself and soon, all too soon, it would just be me. I was terrified, concealing my fears from staff with an air of confidence I did not feel but snappy with Joyce and short tempered with the children. It was Joyce who pulled me round.

"Calm down, for goodness sake, you're driving me nuts. If you didn't want the job you shouldn't have taken it. Dick Adams and the managers obviously think you're up to it."

Did he? Or was it Joyce he wanted? I had a sudden onset of the green-eyed monster. Dick Adams was a charismatic person who some, at least, of the ladies swooned over. Was I just a part of the package? What had they talked about in two hours at camp? I didn't ask, but as though she was reading my thoughts – and she probably was – Joyce started to tell me. It was clear that they had ranged over a wide spectrum of topics and that they had got on very well together but somehow my foolish jealousies disappeared. When she told me that Dick Adams thought we had a great future together in the Approved School Service I was absurdly pleased, and went back to work with renewed vigour. We said our farewells to Bill Hall as he set off for the Continent, and girded our loins for three weeks of our new responsibilities.

The first weekend was a doddle. Byron and Wesley houses were at peace and Carpenter House had an outing to the local cinema. There was some trouble in the toilets with local Teddy Boys, which threatened to escalate, but Bertie Boast, the housemaster, stamped on it before it got out of hand. Sunday to Tuesday passed without incident. I was up and around the school at the crack of dawn and throughout the day and staff and boys were at peace, but I was aware of an undercurrent of excitement and my antennae began to twitch. There was an indefinable air of mystery, which was made clear by the conversation with Desmond. I checked the facts with Phillip, my erstwhile tormentor but now strong support, who was within a few weeks of being licensed and much too intelligent to be involved in such a crackpot scheme as that outlined by Desmond.

"You won't have any trouble, Sir. They'll be glad of an excuse to drop out."

"Well, we'll soon see. Ring the school bell for fire drill."

It was not unknown for the school bell to be rung in mid-afternoon but on that Wednesday in January 1957 the drill did not follow the normal pattern of a brief word of congratulation for a quick response and then back to work. As usual, everyone was directed into the assembly hall. As usual, chairs had been set out and everyone was told to sit. What was not usual was that Dick Adams came through the door.

"Do you mind if I join you, Mr Stanway?" Polite as ever.

"Of course not, Mr Adams. Sit where you wish."

"Thank you. I'll sit at the back."

What could be going on? I stopped the buzz of conversation, not without a wry recollection of a very different Wednesday just over a year ago, and turned towards the stage where there was a little heap of objects covered by a blanket. With a theatrical gesture I whipped the blanket aside to reveal a stock of home-made weapons. I picked up a rather crudely shaped rounders bat with two six-inch nails driven through the head at right angles and waved it menacingly about.

"What would happen if I hit someone with this?"

"They could be dead, Sir."

Indeed they could.

I picked up a large bolt with two substantial nuts locked together at the opposite end to the head with a gap of five inches or so between them bound round with insulation tape.

"Not much use as a weapon, is it?"

"Oh yes, Sir," said some obliging boy. "It's like a knuckle-duster."

"Show me."

Half a dozen boys were ready to oblige.

"You hold it in your fist like this with the nuts sticking out then you can hit someone with it. We read about it in an American comic."

I invited Raymond, who like Phillip was about to be licensed, to take one and hit me on the head. I was glad he didn't – I would have had to take rapid evasive action – but everyone could see that, at the very least, I would be severely injured.

At that point I revealed that I knew all about the proposed fight with the Eastville gang on Saturday.

"That is why we've interrupted your work. That is why we have this special assembly. That is why I invited Mr Adams to be here." I paused for full effect.

"There will be no fight on Saturday."

I fulminated about the possible consequences of such a fight, painting such a lurid picture of blood and gore that even Desmond could not fail to understand the scale of possible disaster.

"We are now going to collect any other weapons anyone has prepared. Providing we get them all there will be no disastrous consequences. Stand up any boy who has weapons anywhere."

Nineteen boys, from all three houses but mostly Carpenter, stood up. It was clear that they were relieved to be found out in an escapade that had rapidly escalated out of control. I sent them off one at a time, accompanied by staff members, to fetch their weapons and in quick time we had an awesome collection. Bats, clubs, sharpened blades, bicycle chains and another four of the unconventional knuckledusters. My final word was to suggest that those involved should not bother to ask for a Saturday pass and I sent everyone off for house meetings.

I had a few words with Dick Adams, who expressed satisfaction with the way it had turned out. We discussed whether to tell Bill Hall, the managers or the police and for each the answer was 'no'. Bill Hall and the managers would find out in due course from a log book entry which would emphasise that, after all, the violence was all in the mind and nothing had really happened outside the school.

"Thank you for what you've done. Leave Bill to enjoy a well earned break."

Though all seemed resolved, I was left a bit bruised and battered at the thought of what could have happened. Over the next few days I talked individually to all the boys involved and was satisfied that, with the possible exception of two very dull Carpenter House boys, they were very happy to be dragged back from the brink of disaster.Nevertheless I reflected that without the information service available to me through the Boys' Committee my tenure as a deputy head could have been the shortest on record.

With mayhem averted we could, we thought, expect a period of relative calm until Bill Hall returned. Home leave was due in a month's time, shortly after Bill Hall's return, and this usually meant a settled period for most boys as they were looking forward to a break. Some, of course, would have apprehensions as to how they would be received at home, though with few exceptions they would be reluctant to admit any such worries to staff or their mates. I could see no storm clouds on the horizon and after the traumas of a few months earlier our marriage was in fine form. Kate, ever the perceptive one, said, "Daddy was singing 'There's a long, long trail a-winding' this morning. He sounded very happy."

"Yes, we all are," said Joyce. "We are enjoying our work and two lovely girls."

The next weekend passed peacefully. No threats from the Eastville gang, no latecomers from Saturday leave, peaceful church services and uninterrupted nights. Dick Adams popped in to see us on Sunday evening to inform us that he would be away in London for three days for meetings at the Home Office. He said he hoped to come back with final approval for the expenditure for a third-in-charge to share senior staff duties.

"Hopefully this will be the last occasion when there will only be one person in charge for such a long period."

We discussed a few practical details, and he reminded us that we would shortly be receiving a Peter Simkins from London. Unusual, but it happened from time to time that youngsters who had caused exceptional difficulties in one region might eventually be transferred to another. No great administrative problem, as Approved School Orders were valid nationwide. I had to admit that I had not read Peter's papers.

"Not surprising, they only came a couple of days ago. They're pretty desperate to get him moved. He's in a police cell at the moment, and the powers that be don't like that. Where will you put him?"

"Oh, Wesley House, that's the only house with a vacancy at the moment."

"I shall be interested to see how he settles. He's been a bit of a handful apparently so they will want him off their hands."

A few more routine matters and Dick Adams said his farewells. "I leave the school in your capable hands."

What a charmer!

As soon as he had gone I said to Joyce that I had better get over to school and read Peter's papers. "If Dick Adams thinks he'll be 'a bit of a handful', we'd better be prepared."

I extracted the papers from the secretary's office. Not even a proper file, just a large sheaf of separate reports with a note to say that the assessment centre summary would be delivered with the boy. Not the best preparation for receiving Peter but at least we had plenty of material to wade through. It appeared that every establishment that had dealt with him had put in its twopenny-worth. Normally the assessment centre or classifying school would give us a succinct summary of previous reports before giving its own balanced view after conducting its own tests.

It soon became clear, as I waded through the mass of papers, that Peter was indeed a difficult boy to deal with. After being in three different primary schools, and excluded from each after violent attacks on other pupils, he had been sent to a junior approved school. His home situation was chaotic – quite a usual story in our experience – father deserted, mother with a succession of partners, truancy, shoplifting and finally a quite vicious attack on a school 'friend' which resulted in his committal. The home situation then improved considerably when mother found a permanent partner and Peter was sent home. Well into secondary age by this time, he was sent to one of the pioneering London comprehensives. Every procedure they could think of to give him a chance was tried – child guidance, extra classroom help, psychological assessment, and treatment in their special unit. All to no avail. He remained stubbornly uncooperative, violent towards his fellows and to staff, and continuing to run riot around his home. He was finally again brought before a juvenile court and a further Approved School Order was made.

I was particularly interested in the reports from his comprehensive. There was a one-page summary by the principal which said, in essence, that he was simply beyond control. In addition he had appended one-page reports from every member of his staff who had had any dealings with Peter. One or two had some constructive comments but in the main they were a catalogue of violence, delinquency and abusive foul language, all with undertones of despair for the future. The one that sticks in my mind was from a PE master who gave a vivid account of meeting Peter for the first time in a gym period, when he was new to the school. Peter was obviously testing his authority from the start.

> *I told the boys to go and sit down, Peter remained standing. I picked out four boys, and told the rest to number off in fours and form teams. Everyone did so except Peter. I stood beside him and told him to join his team. He said, "Fuck off." Not then being used to such language I pushed him outside and told him to report to his form master.*

A further court appearance, inevitably another Approved School Order, re-assessment and placement in an intermediate approved school in the Home Counties... and so the dismal catalogue continued. Absconding, further offences, and finally the agreement by Dick Adams that we should give him a trial at Kingswood. He had stabbed a policeman with a flick knife when he was arrested and was now held in a police cell pending his transfer to us. There could be no guarantee that we could do any better than his previous establishments; he was almost certainly one of those who, in due time, would progress through the system to Borstal and probably prison, but in the meantime we had to give him a try. I gave the Wesley House staff a brief summary of his background and we awaited his coming with some apprehension but with resignation. He would not be the first very difficult boy we had taken in.

I asked John Briers, our clinical psychologist, to prepare a tentative treatment programme, pending the official summary from the London assessment centre. "We need that before we can deal with him properly. I've asked them to give us at least a few days to look at the papers before we take him."

Privately I was hoping that both Dick Adams and Bill Hall would be back before Peter arrived. I did not fancy dealing with him myself. I would have Dick Adams's support in three days and Bill Hall's in eleven, so I was determined to stall as long as possible. If the process followed the usual police pattern with absconders we would be asked to arrange an escort to collect Peter. That would at least make it possible to delay a couple of days until Dick Adams returned. One could imagine all kinds of problems and it would be useful to have someone of such vast experience around.

The bad news came when I arrived back to the office after my mid-morning look at the classrooms. My secretary informed me that there was a message from the police in London to say that they were delivering Peter Simkins to the school the following day. They did not require any transport: they were coming by train to Temple Meads station and had arranged with the Bristol police to be taken on to Kingswood. Two police officers were detailed to do the escorting and would deliver

Peter direct to the school. I was horrified. I knew instinctively that for Peter to be brought to school in that way would be disastrous for him, and extremely difficult for the school. He would without any doubt be seen as the 'big chief' who required two policemen to deal with him. I rang the number the police had left and had a long and increasingly acrimonious conversation with the inspector in charge of the arrangements. He was adamant. "It is our duty to deliver him safely to you – he's a violent absconder."

I pointed out that we were an open institution, and that he could abscond freely as soon as the police left.

"Well that will be your responsibility not ours. As soon as you sign for him he's off our hands."

I was up against a brick wall of officialdom and could see no way forward. I considered ringing the Home Office to talk to Dick Adams and immediately rejected the idea. It was, after all, some high official in the Home Office who had authorised the transfer. I thought of ringing the good Brigadier, who was temporary chairman of the managers while the chairman was on holiday, but could see no purpose in it. I consulted John Briers, who agreed absolutely with me that it would be disastrous but could offer me no useful way forward. For once even Joyce could suggest nothing and then the solution came to me – I thought of the final words of the inspector: "As soon as you sign for him he's off our hands…"

No doubt at all, I would be exceeding my authority, but I was determined to go down fighting. Gathering my resolve, I rang London again. The gist of my conversation this time was simple – I was not going to sign for Peter in the school. I offered a face-saver. "I will pick him up myself from Temple Meads, and sign for him there. Your officers will then have discharged their duty."

The inspector didn't like it, but in the end I left him no choice and, with obvious reluctance, he agreed, providing I signed to say that I accepted full responsibility from the time they put him in the car. "Make sure you bring at least one other member of staff. The boy's violent."

And so in due course I appeared at Temple Meads station to meet the 2.30pm express from Waterloo, apprehensive but trying manfully not to show it and totally convinced that I was doing the right thing. At least the police were in plain clothes and Peter was not in handcuffs. I thought of all the reports I had read, but when I looked at this somewhat unkempt, unhappy, clearly apprehensive fifteen-year-old I had difficulty fitting the facts to the person. With a flash of inspiration I asked if they had managed refreshments on the train – they hadn't!

"Well then, lets go to the refreshment room and have a bite to eat."

Peter made short work of a sandwich, a cream bun and a glass of coke, and the officers certainly enjoyed the break and the snack. I was not so sure about enjoying the refreshments – I was too wound up – but I think I concealed my anxieties. I signed the papers accepting responsibility, we shook hands and the four of us walked, as though we were just good friends seeing each other off, back to my car on the forecourt. Peter sat in the front passenger seat, not even a seat belt in those days to restrain him, and before we set off I gave him some information about the school and the words of encouragement I was quite used to giving to new boys – new start, putting the past behind them, new opportunities and so on. He could easily have run away at that point, so the first little victory was that he didn't. The second was that I was obviously putting trust in him. He was clearly surprised that I was on my own.

"The police said there would be two people to pick me up."

"Why?", I said, pretending surprise.

No answer.

"I did think of bringing my wife so that she could meet you but she's busy with our two little girls."

And so with more such inconsequential chat we made our way back to school. Once there, without any trouble or bad language but with little real contact, I delivered him over to the house staff to be kitted out. His minimal possessions, one small carrier bag, were deposited in his locker and without any demur he had a shower and put on the clean clothes his house matron had provided for him. So far so good. If he ran away now it would have been no different from what it could have been had the police brought him right to the school. He would be just another ordinary runaway and not the great desperado who needed two police to deal with him.

I wrote the whole episode up in the logbook and went home, mightily relieved but under no illusions about the future. There would obviously be troubles ahead but at least we had made a good start. I thought we might have at least a few days of peace – wild optimism! At 7.30am the following day there was an urgent knocking on our front door, and an excitable Wesley House boy. Joyce went to the door; I was shaving.

"Mr Mumbery says can Sir come at once, the new boy's having a head fit!"

I shouted from the bathroom, "I heard – tell Mr Mumbery I'll be there as soon as I can."

Remember the drill, Stanway; take your time, remember PC Plod. Don't rush. Stay calm. Give it time to settle.

Into the house. A little crowd of boys waiting to see what's going to happen. Upstairs to the new boy's bedroom, half a dozen boys looking excited. Peter still in bed, with Mr Mumbery looking agitated beside it. What to do? Clear everyone out except

Mr Mumbery, that would be the normal procedure. Why did I not do it? I'll never know, for I acted purely on instinct. Standing beside the bed, I barked out a no-nonsense command.

"Come on Peter, don't be silly. Get up."

"Fuck off."

Without any conscious thought I got hold of the bed, the usual metal, hospital-type three-foot single, and tipped it upside down, depositing Peter on the floor.

"All right now boys. You've all had your fun, downstairs for a wash."

What I would have done if Peter had repeated his defiance I do not know, but he meekly followed the rest downstairs and relative harmony was restored. I took him out from breakfast to the office. What he expected me to do I don't know. He seemed surprised when I was not shouting at him but talking quietly, more in sorrow than in anger. I told him that so far as I was concerned the incident was closed.

"It's your first full day here. Come and see me after school this afternoon and tell me what sort of a day you've had."

I pondered for a while whether I could have dealt with the matter differently and could come up with no better answer. I was not proud of what I had done but we had re-established, at least temporarily, a hierarchy which Peter and the other boys recognised and with which we could happily co-exist.

When Brigadier Johnson visited a few days later, I put him and Dick Adams fully in the picture. They unequivocally supported my action in not having the police escort Peter to the school. It remained an open question whether the support would have survived had Peter run away on his way to school, but that's life. I never did have much interest in those television programmes about the 'What ifs' of history. What if Harold had not received an arrow in his eye? So what?

It would be a nice rounding off to the Peter saga if I could have reported him a success in life, but reality is not always so accommodating. He did settle down with us without absconding or committing any serious attacks on staff or his fellows and eventually, after a turbulent few months, we licensed him a few days after his sixteenth birthday to go home. We did not see him back in school, but regretfully he finished up in Borstal and we lost contact.

Bill Hall returned from his three-week holiday refreshed and raring to go ahead with changes to school routine that had been in the pipeline for some time but had been put on hold because of the departure of his previous deputy. It was a good time for change. The housemaster and housemother in Byron House had moved on, and the power base in the house had moved away from Phillip and his cronies. In any case, Phillip was leaving on licence as soon as suitable arrangements for his future could be agreed with his parents. The new houseparents were relatively inexperienced in the residential field but were full of enthusiasm and a capacity for hard work that promised well for the future.

This was a time of considerable expansion in the Approved School Service. New schools were being opened and existing ones expanded to cope as the numbers of youngsters being committed by the juvenile court continued to rise. The pressure for places was such that the training school's certified number had been temporarily increased from 120 to 135. The strain on the school's staffing, as on living and teaching accommodation, was considerable. Soon after Bill Hall's return we had a senior staff meeting with Dick Adams to plan various changes – they were going to be quite sweeping, involving considerable building work and a wholesale revision of the disciplinary framework of the school.

It was clear from the discussion that Bill Hall had known quite clearly what had been going on in Byron House and had not liked it.

"Why did you not tackle it head on then?"

"All sorts of reasons, but mainly we wanted to see how you tackled it."

"But I didn't tackle it. I couldn't without outside help and I nearly broke under the strain."

"Yes, well – you didn't break down and now we can work together."

That was as much explanation as I could get. The truth, as I realised when I thought of my own experiences in secondary modern school and in running youth clubs, is that whenever you devolve power downwards in an organisation it is all too easy for rogue elements to take control. It was obvious when I considered the power set-up in Byron House that a small group of intelligent boys had manipulated the system in such subtle ways, and with such small increments of power, that casual observers did not even recognise the changes. And of course it was much easier for staff to go along with the system than try to change it. Indeed this could only have been achieved by a concerted effort by all staff working in the house.

Dick Adams made some encouraging remarks about the boys' club, with its emphasis an corporate responsibility, and invited Bill Hall and I to consider to what extent we could incorporate these ideals into the general framework of the school. This would form part of a radical rethink of school policy, which moved us further away from the old idea of approved schools as merely punishment regimes and towards the concept of an educational institution. To this end he invited us to produce a new 'Rewards and Privileges' scheme that could be agreed by all staff and made known to the boys, giving them clear goals to aim at and clear markers as to their progress. We were asked to produce draft proposals for consideration and comment by all staff within a fortnight.

The building work within the school had been on the radar for some time. All sorts of ideas had been put forward and were now, according to Dick Adams, about to be agreed by the Home Office. The plans were radical. All the large areas in the houses were to be split into smaller units. No more dormitories for up to forty boys, with serried ranks of uniformly arranged beds, but bedrooms for two, three or four boys, arranged along a central corridor. The dining room for one hundred and twenty boys was to be split into three sections and there were to be major changes to the office accommodation. The open colonnades along the front of the school were to be filled in to give us, at a stroke, much increased accommodation for classrooms, offices and extra dining space.

The good news was that we were to be given the necessary money providing the work could be done by the trade training departments in the school. The department instructors, Norman Oxley for stonemasonry and building, Jack Horsman for painting and decorating and Howard Poolman for carpentry and woodwork, were not only willing but very keen to be given something so practical and worthwhile to do.

On top of the building projects and the disciplinary changes, we learned that were to have extra staff, including, finally, a third-in-charge who would share overall supervision with Bill Hall and myself. We would be on full duty one weekend in three instead of two, and future holidays would be arranged so that there would always be two of us left to share duties – what bliss! Dick Adams also informed us that the certified number of the school was eventually to be reduced from 120 to 105, thirty-five boys to each house instead of forty.

All these changes had come about as a direct result of a visit by Home Office inspectors, which concluded, in essence, that we were doing an excellent job but that our staffing and facilities were not up to modern standards. This was something that Dick Adams had been saying ever since he arrived at Kingswood but the Home Office mills grind slowly, especially where considerable extra money is required. One great help in getting the changes agreed was the standard achieved in our trade training departments. Their workmanship and finished results were of such quality that all the building changes could be carried out as training opportunities for the department boys.

I had not been active in the planning stages for the construction projects but now, as deputy head, I was to be involved. Not as clerk of works, that would be way beyond my practical skills, but I was charged by Bill Hall with seeing that the instructors had the supplies they needed and that they kept within the financial limits they had worked out for themselves. As it turned out the latter was not a problem – Norman Oxley, the building and stonemasonry instructor who was to be responsible for the major part of the work, had put in the estimates, which, though well below the cost of outside constructors, made very generous provisions for materials. Labour, always the major cost in such work, was of course free.

The work started without delay and would continue for the best part of two years. It might have been expected that the dust and dirt and inevitable disruption to normal routine would have been upsetting to boys and staff, but right from the start the opposite was the case. Instead of what sometimes seemed pointless training exercises, building practice walls of brick and stone in the workshop and then knocking them down again, the stonemasonry and building department was constructing walls which were to last indefinitely. As each piece of work was finished the painting and decorating department moved in to finish things off.

While all this work was going on we were busily appointing new staff. We had one teaching vacancy following the departure of my predecessor, another to take the place of Bob Kenny, my next-door neighbour at home and in the classroom who had moved to the classifying school as deputy head, and we had been granted an additional teaching appointment. We were to have two new social workers to work with John Briers. We were also to have the previously unimagined luxury of having all the hours between lights-out in the houses and the boys getting up in the morning covered by night supervisors, one just for the training school and a second to be shared with the classifying school. They were to do routine patrols through the bedrooms, cover incoming phone calls and deal with any minor emergencies. Granville Bird was appointed specifically to the training school, and soon proved to be a caring and reliable member of staff, liked and trusted by the boys.

John Inkley was appointed to take over my form in the classroom and, with his family, moved into the next-door house. His experience was well matched to the job and our families soon became good friends. But most exciting from my point of view was the appointment of Theo Griffiths. He was to take over Bob Kenny's form and was in due course to become third-in-charge. This meant that there would always be two people available for overall cover.

Theo and I got on well from the start. We were both practising Methodists but apart from that were very different in experience and capabilities. His teaching experience was in an ESN school in Bristol and he was brilliant at devising courses for special needs children. Apart from one year in Derbyshire with a remove form, my experience and inclinations were geared to the upper streams.

Even more important from our point of view at Kingswood, Theo had the practical skills in woodwork, metalwork and home maintenance that I lacked. We fitted well from the start and became not just colleagues but lifelong friends. When in due course he was appointed as third-in-charge there was an immediate alteration to weekend duty rotas so that Bill Hall, myself and Theo alternated, working one weekend in three.

By mutual agreement we did not alter senior staff cover for the boys' home leaves. For my remaining years at Kingswood I was on duty for all home leave periods since Joyce, as deputy matron, was always on duty to cover the house matrons, who took a holiday with their husbands while the boys were away. The arrangement suited everyone. The home leaves were generally quite pleasant times, with few boys in school and a very relaxed regime operating, but there was always the possibility of minor crises arising. It might be a homesick boy in school, missing his mates, not understanding why his parents don't want him at home and perhaps being teased by other boys quite happy to be in school and reducing him to tears by their ridicule. The first time this happened I was astonished to see Joyce pitching into the tormentors with a scathing tongue-lashing before taking the tearful boy into the office for a consoling hug.

I realised at that point that Joyce had advantages in dealing with boys that were denied to me. With no disciplinary power other than the force of her personality it was so unusual for boys to see her letting drive at them that when it happened it always worked. One factor was her size – five foot nothing if she stretched to her full height – which never inhibited her from tackling, verbally, sixteen-year-olds who could have picked her up and thrown her across the room. The crucial difference between Joyce and me, however, was that when the storm was over she could take a tearful, tormented, homesick boy on the side and give him a caring, motherly hug. The other important factor was that she made it clear, once peace was re-established that the incident was closed and that no one would be referred to me for any further action.

CHAPTER 7

The Joyce effect!

One of the benefits of our new situation when we started working together was the immediate, and by our standards considerable, improvement in our finances. With no mortgage to pay and a very low rent for our pleasant house we had been comfortable enough before, but now, with Joyce's salary and the extra allowance for the deputy head's post, we could afford to branch out somewhat. We had to pay for Mrs Jepson to look after Christine on a regular basis when Joyce had to be in school on her own, and we continued to pay Lyn as a baby-sitter on a regular basis. We also began, looking ahead to the time when we would no longer be in residential work, to make regular contributions to unit trusts, sufficient eventually, we hoped, to cover the purchase of a house.

In a rash moment we handed in our Ford Popular car in part exchange for a second-hand Zephyr Six convertible. Not a very practical buy. It had an electrically operated soft top which severely limited the boot space, and bench seats which could never, however much we tried, be satisfactorily adjusted to suit both my six feet two and Joyce's five foot nothing. If the front seat was adjusted for Joyce I couldn't get my knees in, and if it was adjusted for me Joyce could not even reach the steering wheel! Eventually it was straightforward enough – Joyce used three large cushions and a massive girl's annual on which she could rest her feet so that she could reach the pedals.

Seating positions aside, it was a superb car to drive and Joyce loved it. She was driving on our first trip in the car up to Derbyshire when we had a minor accident. We were following a learner driver in an old Austin 7, and Joyce stayed well behind him because he was driving erratically. We came to traffic lights at a cross roads and pulled up a good twenty yards behind the learner. Unfortunately he had stalled and couldn't get started. His mate got out to give him a push but the car ran away from him and cannoned, quite gently, into us. I could see no damage to our car but there was a considerable dent in his rear end. We had a similar accident when I was driving in Luxembourg and had stopped to peacefully admire the lovely view. There was a considerable bang behind – a 2CV had run into our rear! Again it was the small car which came off much the worst. The Zephyr was built like a tank, with its substantial chassis and general air of solidity, and its excellent six-cylinder engine made it a pleasure to drive. We got rid of it, however, after an incident with Christine. We were bowling merrily along with the hood fully down when Joyce said, "Pull over slowly and carefully."

"Why?"

"Never mind, just do it."

Christine, tired of doing nothing in particular, had climbed over the back and was halfway over the boot with Kate hanging grimly on to her reins. We pulled her back in and put the hood up to the halfway point. We were sad to see the car go but exchanged it for a new Ford Anglia.

More important than the extra money or higher status of our new jobs was the simple fact that we were now working together. It was the start of a happy and fruitful working partnership that was to last twenty-nine years and take us through to retirement, but there were rocky patches in the early months, which caused serious glitches in our relationship. The trouble, as I saw it, was that as soon as Joyce had access to the boys' files and read what were often horrific stories of family neglect and cruelty, she became in my view too emotionally involved. I felt that with my position as deputy head I had to establish my authority, and could not afford to let the heart rule the head. I was still, to a degree, haunted by the memory of my early disasters in Byron House. As time progressed and I became increasingly confident in my ability to control the group, I could move closer to Joyce's viewpoint and accept her arguments on behalf of her troubled boys without fearing disciplinary chaos resulting. Eventually we were recognised by staff and boys as a solid working partnership. It was a strength rather than a weakness when we reached the stage where we could have vigorous arguments in staff meetings, formal or informal, and come amicably to an agreed course of action.

One of the boys with whom Joyce very quickly formed a close bond was Darrell. She was encouraged to do so by the Wesley House team and by John Briers, our psychologist. There was nothing to lose, since no one so far had achieved any real breakthrough with this intelligent, but deeply troubled, boy. We were very near the end of the road, and if he continued on his now well-established pattern of absconding and committing offences he was inevitably Borstal-bound.

Joyce was perhaps his last hope at Kingswood. She played chess with him and asked him for help when she was on relief house duty, but put him under no pressure to talk and asked no awkward questions. Under this gentle regime the dam broke, and he opened up to her about his parents. His mother whom he had loved, who had deserted the home when he was seven; his father, also loved, who was often away from home as a commercial traveller; and, crucially, his stepmother Sandra. His attitude to her was complex, according to Joyce. He had, in the past, complained that she had sexually abused him but no one, not even his father, had believed him.

"Is that it? It's all well known, it's in his file."

"No it's not all, not according to Darrell, it got worse on the last home leave."

The story, as Joyce now passed it on to me, was that Sandra had come into the bathroom while he was bathing.

"She had a dressing gown half open and started to wash my back. Then she started on the front and put soap all over me. I had an erection and she masturbated me...

"Later on she came into my bedroom and we had sex. She said, 'There you are Darrell you liked that, so don't tell Dad. I've done it to give you experience.' I don't want it to happen again. It's just not right."

When Joyce told Darrell that she would have to pass on the gist of the conversation to me he agreed reluctantly but begged her to make it clear that he did not want any further action taken. "It will only make matters worse..."

"Well that's his story," said Joyce, "and I believe him."

Did I? At that time I had not knowingly encountered abuse cases in the youngsters I had dealt with in secondary modern school or in day-to-day living. A few mutterings and mumblings perhaps from time to time but I had never followed them up. There was a general tendency in the 1950s to sweep such stories as did appear under the carpet – not to be discussed in polite society. I was so naïve that, while I could certainly visualize 'dirty old men' perverting, or attempting to pervert, children of either sex, I simply could not come to terms with the idea of mature women sexually abusing young boys. And as for a stepmother – surely not!

Joyce, more realistic though still profoundly shocked at Darrell's revelations, was fully convinced that the boy was telling the truth. I was in a quandary. Allegations had been made in the past and, according to reports, been thoroughly followed up by the children's department. The conclusions had been clear enough: Darrell was so anti-stepmother and so tied to his mother that he was prepared to do anything to break up his father's marriage, cherishing the hope that if only he could achieve that his parents would inevitably get together again.

It is difficult now, looking back over the years, to fully understand the hush-hush atmosphere which surrounded stories of sexual abuse. We know now that there were cases of systematic sexual abuse of youngsters in care homes and various residential institutions which were, at the time, dismissed as the imaginings or, worse, wicked lies of disturbed youngsters. We know now that some cases were hushed up. With the wisdom of hindsight it is easy to be critical of actions taken at the time. Proof was not easy to find when of necessity it was the word of children against staff, and it was certainly possible for youngsters to make up stories. With my limited experience at the time it was easier for me to accept the judgement of experienced staff who had spoken to Darrell about his allegations than to accept the monstrous thought that his allegations might be true. I passed on my conclusions to Joyce and she was deeply upset. This was near the start of our full working relationship. If I was right did it mean that she could no longer trust her own judgement on such a vital matter? I made matters worse by telling her to let it rest and just to get on with her routine work.

"Are you saying that that's what my work is to be? Seeing to laundry, checking the kitchen, organising the domestic staff and cooking your evening meal? I thought my job was more than that."

"Of course it's more than that. It's your contact and influence on boys which is most important, but you must take note of what experienced folk have said about Darrell."

"But Darrell says they just didn't listen when he was talking to them before. They just believed her."

The discussion went on but it became clear we were going to get nowhere. Joyce believed Darrell and I, not alone according to the file, believed he was a manipulative liar. At least, said Joyce, someone should see Sandra before Darrell went on home leave in three weeks time. I pointed out that for that to happen we'd have to tell Bill Hall and the house staff and that Darrell had forbidden that.

"Well I'll go back to Darrell and tell him that he must let me pass information on."

"Not till we've given it further thought, give it a rest for a few days. We're out for a meal and the theatre, forget it."

We duly had our meal out – eaten in somewhat frosty silence, and went on to see a Brian Rix farce. In the circumstances it was just about the worst choice we could have made. The dropping of trousers, the double entendres and the continual sexual innuendos simply reminded Joyce of what she now believed to be Darrell's torment. In the interval Joyce, to my intense annoyance raised the matter again.

"Do you know the worst thing about Darrell and Sandra?"

"I don't want to know but I expect you're going to tell me."

"No, no I can't. I promised Darrell I wouldn't."

We left the theatre without seeing the second act and went home early. We sent Lyn home, had a hot drink and went to bed. I put my arms round my beloved and whispered in her ear. There was no response and when I looked at her face it was wet with tears. I was stricken.

"What's the matter, what have I done?"

"It's not to do with you, it's Darrell."

"That's ridiculous, you're getting too involved with that boy. Forget it – at least till tomorrow – let it rest."

Rest was what we were not going to have. I got up and made a drink of hot chocolate but it didn't help. Tears continued.

"For heaven's sake, get it off your chest."

A slight smile at that.

"I've got nothing on my chest at the moment."

"You know what I mean..."

I was losing patience. We got up, donned dressing gowns and went downstairs. I sat in a comfortable armchair and Joyce put a cushion on the carpet and leaned against me. Gradually, but with increasing confidence, she began to fill in the details of Sandra's seduction of Darrell. I couldn't see anything new.

"You've told me that before. Why should that affect our married life? There must be something else you haven't told me."

"There is. When Darrell had sex with Sandra, he enjoyed it. Now he's full of guilt but he's afraid that if he goes home and Dad's away it will happen again, and he won't be able to help himself."

"Well he's sixteen, his hormones are raging. It's not surprising he enjoyed it."

"Oh for heaven's sake you just don't get it do you. Suppose you had sex with your stepmother."

"I haven't got a stepmother."

"Oh for God's sake use your imagination. Think of our courtship, and the first time we made love. All those wonderful experiences we have shared which Darrell can never have."

"Why can't he? He's a bright lad, he'll meet a nice girl and put this behind him."

"Oh Jesus wept! You're supposed to be intelligent. The spectre of Sandra would always come between them."

No one, to my knowledge, at that time talked of 'post traumatic stress' but that's what Joyce, with a skill born of her instinctive empathy, was talking about without being able to put a name to it.

We talked on into the small hours. She told me, apropos of nothing at all, of an incident which happened while I was away in the army. Her dad had a senior position with the Woolwich Arsenal as a quality controller and had been assigned to an armaments firm that had been bombed out of Birmingham and taken over a local factory in Langley Mill, Derbyshire. He had recruited and trained a group of local ladies to form an independent inspection panel checking the anti-aircraft and other shells produced. Joyce accompanied her father regularly as a consort at various official functions when her mother would not attend. One of the factory bosses took Joyce and her dad to a dinner dance in Nottingham.

"We danced together several times and he started pitching me the classic tale of marital troubles, a wife who didn't understand his needs. 'Perhaps we can get together on our own sometime. I know a good hotel – good food, good accommodation.'"

"What a corny line. What did you tell him?"

"I said I'd ask my dad to let him know when my fiancée was coming on leave from the army. Perhaps we could all get together. I didn't hear any more but when we got in his chauffeur-driven car for the drive home I sat in the front, so that the two men could talk business in the back."

Where did my sweetheart learn such sophisticated wiles? Certainly not from her mother. And not from me. Compared to Joyce I was naïvety personified.

We talked on and came to no conclusions. I was, in spite of all my doubts and my common-sense approach, coming to believe that Joyce's assessment was right and that the professionals who had summarily dismissed Darrell's complaints as malicious lies were wrong. I had some serious thinking to do. In the meantime Joyce had challenged me on another front.

"Think of our courtship and marriage and you might understand my concerns for Darrell. He can never know the joys that we have had, and may still have."

"That's stretching it a bit."

"Is it? Think about it."

I had a sudden thought, and back-tracked.

"Did you say '*may* still have'? Why *may*?"

"Oh stop picking me up on odd words, of course it's *may*. Who can tell what tomorrow will bring, let alone next week, or next year."

With that we made another drink and went to bed. Tears had stopped but making love was not on the menu. I tossed and turned, wondering how on earth I was going to tackle Darrell's problems. Finally I slept uneasily. My last conscious thoughts were of Joyce and our courtship. If Joyce wanted me to think about it I would.

. . . . .

I first met Joyce in February 1941 when she came with her parents to the Methodist church I attended. She was two months from her sixteenth birthday.

We were introduced by our Sunday school superintendent as we were to be in the same senior class. All that the rest of us knew at the time was that her parents were renting a house just round the corner from us and that she was joining them. She was reticent about her background and it was a week or two before we knew anything of her history. When we did it seemed to us, in our still peaceful backwater, positively glamorous.

Born in County Durham, moved to London at the age of nine, evacuated to Maidstone in 1939, to grandparents in County Durham in 1940, back to London, bombed out, back to Durham and eventually to Heanor, Derbyshire. I looked at her in some awe – beautiful but beyond reach.

My experience of girls at that time was, to say the least, limited. It's true that I was in a mixed grammar school but boys and girls, so far as I was concerned, just did not mix. Part of the reason was my totally unbalanced physical development. I was seventeen years and a few months, six feet two in height, not much over ten stones in weight and had only recently come into some sexual maturity. I had been a boy soprano singing in local musical festivals until just before my sixteenth birthday, and it would be years before I needed to shave regularly. I don't think I was shy with girls, just indifferent to their undoubted charms. I could hold my own academically – I was habitually top of the form in examinations – but as the eldest of six from a financially poor family I was very much the odd one out throughout my school days. If the stories of sexual shenanigans behind the bike shed were true, boys with boys or boys with girls, they had certainly passed me by. I had had a weekend away at the local conference centre with a girl from Sunday school, but it was a Scripture Union training course and when we went for a walk we didn't even hold hands. No, so far as girls were concerned, I was a *tabula rasa*, so when this ravishing newcomer took an interest in me as a friend it was like a lightning bolt. It was the sudden awakening of sex – I was moonstruck!

We talked and talked about life, religion, politics, the brave new world after the war, families, ambitions, hope and fears. I had cycled to both London and Durham in school holidays, so knew something of her past haunts. We got on well as friends; how long it would have taken me to go any further than that, I will never know, but three people decided to move things along rather more quickly. The first was my Aunty Annie, who lived with us. She told me that Joyce was a lovely girl and that she obviously liked me. "Ask her out, you've got some money." I did have money – I had always had spare time jobs from the age of twelve and from my fifteenth birthday I had been earning up to thirty-five shillings a week collecting for a rediffusion company. A pound was a much-needed boost to household expenses, but the rest, up to fifteen shillings a week in my pocket, was riches indeed.

I still hesitated, and then Joyce herself decided some action was needed. We had one of our regular church socials for youngsters and one of the daft games played was 'Postman's Knock'. I'm not even sure now how it was played (surely it's not played any more!), but it was popular in our youth and provided some harmless fun. Girls and boys were numbered off separately. It was supposed to be secret but some simple arithmetic could give away the identities. Wonder of wonders, when Joyce was installed as the postman she called out my number from the choir vestry, and I had to go out.

"You are supposed to kiss me now."

So I did. Six foot two and five foot nothing and yet we managed a chaste kiss. A very long way from connubial bliss but it was at least a minor milestone. Aunty was pleased!

Next week I was invited to tea at Joyce's home, not alone – that would have been too forward – but along with another boy and girl who were known to us as 'going out'. I finally cottoned on to the fact that Joyce liked me as a friend, and might even countenance 'boy' in front. I began to take some simple steps to improve our acquaintance. She was at that time working in the offices of a local textile and hosiery firm and walked to work by the same route I walked to school. I hovered each day outside her house and we walked together. Was it I who held her hand first, or was it Joyce who held mine? Whatever – we soon became recognised as a couple.

The third person who moved things along was Joyce's mum, Jenny. Shorter than Joyce, plumpish but attractive and always immaculately dressed and coiffeured, she had an excellent contralto voice and was already a valued choir member in the church. She was always pleasant to talk to unless the subjects of sex or alcohol came up. Alcohol was off limits because she had been a Rechabite from her youth; and Joyce told me later that sex had been a no-go area from 1925 after Joyce was born. She still shared a bed with Joyce's dad, Tom, but that was all. She had had a difficult pregnancy and birth with Joyce and it was something never to be repeated. She had rejected Joyce completely after birth for nine months, and the poor lass had been looked after by Tom's mother.

It was astonishing in these circumstances that Jenny took to me but she did. After that first rather strained teatime, it was she who twice more, two weeks in succession, invited me to Sunday tea before we went together to evening service. I don't know what she intended, but if she had hoped to bring us closer together it had the opposite effect. Joyce was furious, and issued an ultimatum: "If you invite Eric again without asking me first I shall not be there." No more tea invitations from Jenny.

The next little step forward to advance our relationship could well have finished it off altogether. It was after evening church and we were to have one of our occasional get-togethers when up to two dozen of us would converge on somebody's house for tea, lemonade, and such delicacies as the strict rationing of the time would allow. We knew this evening would be a bit special because the couple we were going to ran a grocery and green-grocer's shop so there would be extras. Joyce, bless her, said it was time people knew we meant something to each other and that we should not go with her mum and dad but instead arrive as a couple.

All was going well. A round table was set out with a selection of goodies, mostly home made, which in 1941 we rarely saw. It was a large room, obviously two knocked together, and we were invited to take a chair. I sat beside Joyce, leaned back to say something to a friend behind me, and the chair collapsed in ruins. Not too much of a disaster. It was obviously weak. "Just put it in the kitchen," said our host. Unfortunately as I edged past the round table I put some weight on the edge. The whole top tilted and at least half the crockery and goodies slid on to the floor before we managed to stop them.

Imagine my embarrassment. Seventeen, my first official date, and twenty or so friends to witness my humiliation. We put the wreckage right as best we could and I stood back, moving away to a place of safety. "Don't touch the piano," somebody wisecracked, "we need it later." This lightened the atmosphere and the evening finished happily for everyone but me, and possibly our hosts, who had lost some of their best china.

We walked home together and Joyce insisted we should take a long way round. Double summertime was in operation but as we got to the local park dusk fell and we paused at a secluded spot. We kissed and then, wonder of wonders, Joyce took my hand and guided it to her breast. I could feel it come to life under her bra, but that was as far as it went and when I made to put my hand inside the bra she gently stopped me.

"Sometime but not now."

We kissed again, "My knees feel weak," said Joyce, "we must go home."

We went down the hill to home murmuring sweet nothings to each other. The humiliation of the evening behind us, we were setting out on a course which would take us we knew not where, but at that moment, though we did not put it into words, we believed that we would journey together.

It was just two weeks or so after my house-wrecking evening that I had what I could best describe now as a 'Mrs Robinson experience'. It was a Saturday and I was rushing around collecting the rediffusion money. I was in a slum area known locally as 'Packman's Puzzle' because door-to-door collectors of any kind had such difficulty in getting their money. I hated the area, not just slums but often dirty and stinking. Mrs Hansel was a shining exception. She was quite old – to me, that is: she could well have been in her mid thirties! – but was smart, well presented and had a voluptuous figure. Her home was always clean and tidy, but she was no better at paying than her neighbours and was rapidly approaching the point at which her radio speaker would be repossessed and her entertainment cut off.

On this Saturday her curtains were drawn. I knocked as usual and she called me in. She had just stepped out of a tin bath on the hearth and was draped in a voluminous towel.

"Come in, I'm quite respectable. Just pass me that chair with my clothes on it."

Gullible, naïve fool that I was I did exactly that, and as I did so the towel slipped down to reveal all.

"Don't be bashful, Eric." How did she know my name? "Come closer, I won't bite."

I was not so naïve that I didn't know what was on offer and I beat a hasty retreat.

Was this why Joyce had told me to look again at our courtship? I thought back to seventeen-year-old Eric and Mrs Hansel and in my mind's eye saw Sandra and Darrell; now I could at least see how easily Darrell's seduction could have happened. My growing conviction that Joyce was right was reinforced. Unfortunately it did not mean that I was any nearer to finding a solution.

Nineteen forty-one was a magical year for Joyce and me. We celebrated her sixteenth birthday in some style; I started preaching. Ridiculously young, still just seventeen. It happened by accident. We went to church as usual for the evening service to find that the preacher planned had been taken ill. The steward came over to me – "We liked the address you gave to the Christian Endeavour, would you give it as a sermon, we'll help with the hymns and the readings." Later I did a full training course as a Methodist local preacher years later and qualified in 1952, but 1941 was when I started.

Now sixteen and to me a vision of sheer delight, Joyce changed her job to become secretary of a girl's grammar school in Nottingham. A big step up. Not brilliantly paid but satisfying and superb experience for her later career. It seemed a very responsible job at such a young age but Joyce was much more mature than me, in spite of my eighteen-month age advantage. For my part I was to enter teacher training college in September at Borough Road in London, quite a prestigious establishment as such colleges went in those days. I hoped to complete a three-year course, two years for a Teacher's Certificate and a further year to finish off a degree.

We had an idyllic August. The threat of invasion still hung over us, though less so than in 1940. Rationing was tight, the Battle of the Atlantic was raging, there were reverses for Britain in Greece and Yugoslavia, but we had the optimism of youth and our courtship was progressing steadily. We roamed the countryside at weekends and on summer evenings and it was in our beloved park where first I had tremulously touched Joyce's bra that we went one step further. Somehow when I put my hand inside her blouse this time her bra was unfastened and

I found her bare breasts. Innocent enough, in all conscience, but when we kissed we were both swept away on a tidal wave of emotion. No actual sexual contact but I felt Joyce tremble against me and when I held her tight we both gave a convulsive shudder and there was a cataclysmic release of tension. If we had known the word it would have been 'orgasm'; to us it was simply love.

"Do you mind?", I said to Joyce, fearful of the answer.

"No, no, no, but how long must we wait to get married?"

Though we had pledged our love before we had never mentioned marriage, but from that moment we knew that was what it would be. Perhaps when I was called up in a couple of years. Joyce would get a wives' allowance to go with her salary. We walked arm in arm to home, making wildly improbable plans but blissfully happy.

Joyce and I were officially engaged shortly after Joyce's eighteenth birthday in 1943, by which point I had received my call-up and was well into the endless series of training postings described elsewhere. I carried off the proposal in the approved fashion, after asking her dad's permission. No problem there, we were already well established as a courting couple. Quite unexpectedly I had received a bonus payment from the army of £32, which I only discovered when I asked the pay corps sergeant for a statement of my balance. I queried the amount, thinking it should have been two pounds and not thirty-two.

"Are you saying we are cheating you?" He called over his lieutenant, who verified that the account was accurate. I didn't argue, and put in a formal request to draw the lot.

Joyce and I visited Nottingham and did a bit of window-shopping for a second-hand ring, all that was available in those days. She was very tactfully looking at rings in the £10 range and took some persuading before she would agree on the three-stone ring at £30. I could see that she loved it and I put it proudly on her finger.

My courtship of Joyce proceeded smoothly through the ups and downs of my service career. Home leaves, with rail travel warrants winging me swiftly home and back, were happy intervals. Joyce's work was going well, we planned our future happily together, and we roamed the Derbyshire countryside whenever time allowed. I had come to terms with my lowly army rank and when I heard of the casualty rates among college contemporaries who had joined the University Air Squadron I was, somewhat guiltily, grateful for my poor eyesight that had kept me out of the unit. I felt a similar reaction when I heard that my Sherwood Forester comrades had taken part, and suffered casualties, in North African landings. I was happy to work where I was put, but was not looking to be a hero.

I was fit enough, as was shown by the fact that on two occasions when there was a family celebration I borrowed a bicycle from a friendly sergeant and rode home for a few hours on a 36-hour weekend pass. The 240-mile round trip was exhausting but worthwhile. I would set off back at around nine o'clock Sunday evening, cycle through the night and arrive back in camp in good time for the first parade on Monday.

On one occasion a friend from Nottingham in the same unit came with me. This time we borrowed the sergeant major's tandem. It should have been much easier, but my friend was quite unused to cycling and was totally exhausted by the time I dropped him off at home. I still had another ten miles to do to Heanor and was pretty near the limit myself. I picked him up on the Sunday evening and I remember well that when we stopped for a rest at Wetherby he collapsed on a grass bank at the roadside and was sick. He suggested I leave him there, still forty-five miles from camp, but we got him on the bike somehow and finally made the camp with just a few minutes to spare. The last five uphill miles from Catterick Bridge to the camp were hellish and by the time we presented our passes at the guardhouse I didn't know which of us was the more exhausted.

In April 1944 I was told by the company sergeant major, with whom I had struck up an unlikely friendship, that there would be no follow-up to the group of Free French I was at present guiding through the radio mechanics course.

"So what will happen to me?"

"Well I don't know, but think about what they will need in France. They'll want experts like us to set up the communications links. You'll get your sergeant's stripes and we'll be off together."

I wasn't sure that I was an 'expert', but I did think about it and didn't like my conclusions. It was a stone wall certainty that the army would need signals units on the beach, and that anyone who could liaise with the locals would be invaluable. I was a natural on all counts. I had done a course with the Sherwood Foresters, twenty-two weeks at signals OCTU, nine weeks battle training with 35 Division in Northumberland and a full radio mechanics course. I was familiar with all the radios in use by the army and could not only operate them but, in theory at any rate, repair them if necessary. Furthermore I spoke fluent French. What better destination could there be for me than France? Well, actually I could think of any number of better destinations. Heanor to be with Joyce; London to finish my teacher training and get my degree; anywhere rather than wading ashore on some French beach.

In practical terms I knew exactly what was likely to happen and when, a few days after my conversation with the sergeant major, I was told that my home leave was being brought forward and would be twelve days rather than a week, I sat down at once and wrote to Joyce to give her the good and bad news.

The good, that I would be seeing her sooner than expected; the bad, that it would be embarkation leave. I was excited, fearful, anxious, but in the end quite determined to do my bit – not that I would have any choice. At least, I thought, the war would soon be over. We all thought then that the Germans were near to defeat and that when the assault came they would soon collapse. We knew that they had already suffered desperate losses in Russia.

When I arrived home it was to find that Joyce's parents were going off for a week's holiday in Rhyl with Steve and Belle, Tom's brother and sister-in-law. We would have the house to ourselves. It was on our first evening together that Joyce dropped a bombshell.

"I want us to make love properly this home leave."

"What do you mean?"

"Oh for heaven's sake, do I really have to spell it out? I don't want to wait any longer before we are properly married."

"We can't get married yet. We've had all that out before."

"Oh please spare me, we can be married in the sight of God."

"We can't do it, what about your parents?"

"Well Dad, I'm sure, knows. He told me to be careful and not take any risks."

"And what about Mum?"

"She knows as well, but she won't talk about it."

Joyce went on to tell me of a conversation with her mum that I found difficult to credit. In an unusual burst of intimacy she had said that we, Joyce and I, had something special between us, a love which she had never had and now it was too late for her. From that time on I had a new and clearer understanding of Joyce's mum. The agonies which constrained her, the bleakness of her marriage, the regrets and now the frustrated dreams.

We saw Joyce's parents off on the bus to Derby where they would catch the train and took our time walking back, suddenly unaccountably shy.

I will draw a discreet veil over the next week. I blush even now to think of the naïvety of a grown man who cycled ten miles to Nottingham and came back with three packets of razor blades because he couldn't find a chemist with a male assistant. I told Joyce and she was furious.

"There's a chemist down the street. John, on his own, what's the matter with that?"

"But he knows us."

"Eric Stanway, if you are ashamed of what we are to do, don't do it. I'm not ashamed."

That set the scene. We had a magical, exquisite week shot through, as the week went on, with the growing realisation that this might well be all the married life we would know. Four good friends with whom I had done my infantry signals training had been killed in a North African landing. Why should I be any different?

Joyce's parents returned. A little surprised perhaps to find that they had a new kettle: we had burned out the other one when we had forgotten we had left it on the gas ring. I believe they must have known what had been happening, for there was a radiance about us which was palpable.

And then, all too soon, the leave was over. Joyce's holiday, graciously granted by her delightful and sympathetic headmistress, ended at the same time, and so we returned to Nottingham together, Joyce to go to work and me to catch the train back to Catterick. We were trying desperately to be brave but ended up both in tears. We did not know when, or even if, we would see each other again. I was going off to join the vast armada assembling in Southern England and thence who knew where.

If this were fiction rather than fact I would have gone bravely off to war to the sound of trumpets, won some kind of glory and returned, wounded but not too badly, perhaps with a glamorous limp, to be comforted in my lover's arms. The reality was anticlimactic. When I arrived back at Catterick it was to find another group of Free French, this time with a sprinkling of Belgians, waiting for me to guide them through yet another twenty-four-week course.

I never did see service abroad. There was a minor scare in 1945, when it was rumoured that our unit might be drafted to the Far East for the final assault on Japan, still fighting a desperate rearguard action after the German surrender in May. I was sceptical and quite blasé about all the rumours – we lived with too many of them – but when I was sent on leave at the beginning of August it was just possible that it could be embarkation leave. And then on 6 August the first atomic bomb was dropped on Hiroshima. Three days later Joyce and I had an excursion into Derbyshire. In Bakewell we joined a small, somewhat ancient country bus, crowded with folk singing and cheering. A second bomb had been dropped on Nagasaki and Emperor Hirohito had announced the surrender of Japan.

. . . . .

Reminiscence of our courtship had been pleasant enough but I could not really see how it could give me any clearer understanding of Darrell's problems. And why, why, why was it suddenly having an effect on our married life? If Joyce was going to take the problems of boys with whom she was working into our bedroom I was not at all sure how I could deal with it. I put these issues to Joyce. With considerable patience, but just a touch of irritation at my obtuseness, she put me on the right path.

"So far as our married life is concerned give it a few days and it will be fine. You didn't think I'd gone off sex for good..."

Keep quiet Eric, don't press it. I obeyed my own unspoken instruction, but the atmosphere had suddenly lightened and my grumpiness had gone.

"But where does Darrell fit in? What's our courtship to do with him?"

"Just suppose," said Joyce, going off at a tangent, "that I had gone to a hotel with that odious Alexander, the factory boss friend of father. He was handsome and rich. Just suppose that a bit of innocent canoodling had gone too far, and we had sex."

"But there wasn't any canoodling, you didn't go with him."

"Oh stone the crows, I know I didn't but suppose I *had* had sex and you had found out. Would you have forgiven me?"

I thought about it. Would I? It was easy enough to answer a hypothetical question.

"Well, yes."

"Yes," said Joyce, "I really believe you would, but would I ever have forgiven myself?

"And what about 'Packman's Puzzle' and Mrs Hansel. What if you had had sex with her? I would certainly have forgiven you, but would you have forgiven yourself?"

Well, would I? The light was dawning.

"Now think of Darrell," said Joyce. "He is tormented, full of guilt but fearing that if he is alone at home with Sandra he will not be able to resist her advances. Worse than that, he's not even sure that he *wants* to resist. And my sorrow for him is that whatever happens to him in the future he can never have the supreme joy that we have had, and will have again."

I noted the 'again' – things really were going to be all right! We now, together, had a clear understanding of Darrell's problems but were no nearer a solution to the problem of the coming home leave. If he went home how did we ensure his safety? If he did not go home, at his own request or forbidden by the school, how did we explain things to father? We agreed that Darrell must be persuaded that at least the senior staff ought to be told of his latest allegations, but what then? We had to deal with the social workers who had followed up the previous allegations and decided, categorically, that they were not true. It was a certainty that Sandra would be as vehement as ever in her denials, that she would be supported, as before, by her husband and that the consequences for Darrell's relationship with his dad could be disastrous.

Joyce saw Darrell, as we had agreed, and persuaded him that senior staff must be told the full story. His housemaster too should know. We had an urgent meeting with Bill Hall, John Briers and Charlie Betteridge, the housemaster, and Joyce went through the circumstances just as Darrell had told her. It came over with such crystal clarity that our doubts were swept away and we all knew it was the truth. I think, as much as anything, it was hearing Joyce use the exact phraseology that Darrell had used, the common words that boys used for the vagina, breasts, masturbation and intercourse. The only 'polite' word Darrell had used was 'penis' but somehow, hearing the account from Joyce using Darrell's words, it came across as the literal truth. We listened, came to no immediate conclusion, but agreed that positive action had to be taken, certainly within a week, since the home leave arrangements had to be completed by then. Just what that positive action was to be we did not really know.

I was delegated to have a discussion with Darrell. I wasn't looking forward to it but I was felt to be the right person since Darrell already knew that Joyce had put me in the picture. I collected him personally from his trade department, reassuring him that I just wanted to sort out the coming home leave.

"You told Mrs Stanway at one point that you didn't want to go home because of problems with your stepmother."

"Yes I did say that, but if it's okay I've changed my mind. I want to see my dad."

"But what about your stepmother?"

"Oh I've got that sorted. Nothing's going to happen this time. I'm bigger than she is and I'll tell her to get lost. And I'll make sure that I keep the bathroom door locked. Unless I'm not to go home at all I've got to cope with the bitch sometime."

"What about what's happened in the past? Shouldn't we do something about that, wouldn't that help?"

"Of course it wouldn't, it would just smash things up with Dad, and I've got to live with them in the end."

It seemed to me that Darrell was taking a responsible view. Whether he would be able to carry it through was another matter, but I was satisfied that he was determined to deal with his stepmother in his own way, and in all the circumstances I thought it was the right way.

I reported back to the meeting and got a mixed reception. John Briers, Charlie Betteridge and Joyce agreed with me, though with no great confidence in the outcome. Bill Hall was unhappy that we were condoning a crime, but in the end agreed that it was the only reasonable way. If we had reported it, the police would not in any case have taken the word of Darrell against that of the parents. Arrangements were made and Darrell duly went off on home leave, after assuring us again that he was quite confident he would not be in any danger from Sandra.

This was to be the first home leave when Joyce and I would be in full charge. Joyce automatically, because the house staff would all be on holiday at the same time as the boys; those seven or eight left would be moved to one house and Joyce would act as relief housemother. Since Bill Hall was also due a holiday, I would be in full charge of the school. Twenty-four hours a day, theoretically, though it would always be possible to leave one of the three remaining teachers or instructors in charge for an hour or two. This would be the pattern for all future home leaves while we were at Kingswood, and despite the long hours they were restful times – not this first one, though, we were both too new in the post to be totally relaxed.

We were just getting used to the routine after a couple of days when we heard from the police that Darrell had run away from home. We feared the worst. Dad was away for three days working and we had little doubt that Darrell had had trouble with Sandra and was escaping her. We expected he would follow his previous absconding pattern, committing a burglary or burglaries and then moving into a hotel for four or five days before giving himself up. Perhaps that was his original intention, for he did break into a house, but this time he returned to the school. He knocked at our door at 9pm. We took him in and heard his story. Apparently he had simply feared the worst when dad left, and run away rather than face his stepmother.

We put him to bed and then spent a good hour discussing what we could do with him, without reaching any sensible conclusions. One unusual, and encouraging, development was that he had changed his mind about staying in a hotel and had come back to school. Even better, he had hitchhiked rather than spending any of the money he had stolen and had handed that over to us to be returned. We decided that Joyce would talk to him at length in the morning.

Straight after breakfast Joyce took Darrell into the house office to get the full picture. She began by telling him that he had let her down, since she had stuck her neck out for him in order to get me and Bill Hall to agree to what he wanted. At one point he broke down and sobbed bitterly. He wanted quite desperately to be home with Dad but Dad had made it clear that he loved Sandra and would never take his first wife back – in any case Darrell's mother had a new life of her own. If he was to be with Dad, he therefore had also to be with Sandra.

"What would happen," said Joyce, "if we made sure that Sandra did not interfere with you as she has done in the past, could you live with that?"

"If you could that would be great, but I don't see how you could do it."

"Neither do I," said Joyce, "but someone's got to talk to Sandra at some time."

Still no satisfactory conclusion, but it became clear that Darrell wanted to go back home for another try and that he needed support. Joyce offered to take him home, and to talk with Sandra. With considerable misgivings on my part, we contacted Darrell's probation officer, who was in touch with the home, and in less than an hour Joyce was off on the fifty-mile trip to Darrell's home. I was on tenterhooks all the time Joyce was away, regretting that I had been weak enough to agree to send her on such an impossible mission. How could she possibly get things sorted with the stepmother? It was late evening when she returned and I could hardly wait to get the full story.

How she managed it I would never know but somehow Joyce had achieved such a good relationship with Sandra that soon they were talking quite intimately – about family life, the difficulties of a second marriage, problems with her husband and his first wife, and the frustrations arising from his frequent absences due to work. She loved her husband but he had lost all interest in sex and she was afraid that he must be taking up with some other woman. They talked at length about the shortcomings of men. When Sandra admitted that she had no evidence of sexual misdemeanours Joyce asked about work.

"That's difficult, he's lost some good orders lately."

"Well that could be the answer," said Joyce. "It needn't be another woman. Problems at work will always put a man off sex."

"I hope you didn't say you knew that from experience," I interjected.

"Well not exactly, but I did know what she was talking about."

Crucially, Joyce had then raised the question of Darrell and at this point Sandra burst into tears. Haltingly at first and then more freely she poured out the whole story, pretty well exactly as Darrell had already told Joyce, of what had happened on the previous home leave. "I swear that nothing happened between us this time and nothing is going to happen again. I'm so ashamed."

"Did you believe her?", I asked.

"Yes I did. She meant what she said."

"Well, how did you finish?"

"I told her that so far as the school was concerned we would not tell the father, and that if Darrell wanted to have another go at home I would leave him after I had a talk with him on my own."

And that's what happened. When Darrell returned she told him that she would leave him at home and that she was sure things would be all right with Sandra, but that the police would need to get a statement about the burglary. She saw his probation officer, gave him a sanitised version of her talk with the stepmother and left him the stolen money in an envelope, along with an account of the burglary as we had it from Darrell. The probation officer did not believe the police would wish to take any further action since there was already an Approved School Order in force.

What surprised me most from Joyce's account of her talk with Sandra was the fact that, in spite of everything she knew had happened between Darrell and his stepmother, she could still not only listen but somehow establish such a rapport that Sandra not only revealed the full story of the last home leave but also gave intimate details of her own marriage problems.

"How did you persuade her to be so open?"

"I don't know. I suppose it helped that she was stricken with remorse. Her tears were genuine, I could tell by the way she trembled when I put my arm around her shoulders."

"How on earth could you bring yourself to do that after what she'd done to Darrell?"

"Well it wouldn't have helped if I'd blasted off at her, would it?"

And that, I suppose, was the key. A compassion which I did not think I could have felt myself but which, I'm sure, was the secret of Joyce's success, not just with Darrell and his stepmother but, over the years, with a long succession of folk, boys and parents, who found in Joyce a true confidante in their times of need.

There was one further important step we had to take. In my judgement Joyce had done a brilliant job, but she had taken decisions without consultation and without fully informing the probation officer responsible for Darrell at home. She had also made promises to Sandra about not informing Darrell's dad. It was easy to visualize a scenario where this could blow up into a nasty conflict later. It could quite easily be argued, for instance, that we had knowingly and wilfully left a boy under our care in a situation of moral danger.

Bill Hall, John Briers and Charlie Betteridge were all on holiday but happily Dick Adams was at home. He readily agreed to see us the following morning and Joyce gave him the full story. He was fully supportive of all the actions Joyce had taken and the assurances that she had given, and went on to make suggestions as to how all this was to be recorded. Just a brief, sanitised account in the file. The offence of burglary had to be recorded, making it clear that police had been informed and the stolen money returned. For the rest, a simple statement that Darrell had been taken home and left to complete his home leave. In due course, when people came back from holiday, we would put them in the picture. In the meantime he thanked and congratulated Joyce for what she had done.

CHAPTER 8

Bits and pieces

Boys' Club Week

One of the great events in the calendar for all boys' clubs affiliated to the national association was Boys' Club Week. There were a number of prominent figures who were prepared to lend their names in support of fund raising. Probably the best known in our time was the singer Frankie Vaughan. He was unstinting in his acknowledgement of the debt he owed to the boys' club he attended, to which he gave credit not only for keeping him out of trouble but for setting him off on his musical career. Through the 1950s and 1960s he kept the club week free of professional engagements so that he could go around the country giving support and encouragement to local clubs. He was inspirational in fund raising and generous with money as well as time.

One year, we at Kingswood were thrilled to be offered part of an afternoon and evening for a visit by Frankie to use in any way we felt fit. I was by that time deputy head, so no longer club leader. Joyce was already well established as assistant matron, but still worked happily in the club when time permitted. I was invited to join the Boys' Committee to discuss plans for the visit but declined on principle. I felt it was up to the club committee to come up with suggestions, which they should put to Bill

Hall and myself if there was a conflict with school procedures. Fortunately these restrictions did not apply to Joyce, who was welcomed in the club as a non-authoritarian figure and duly invited to join in a committee meeting.

It was clear from the start that this was going to be a big event. Frankie was at the height of his popularity and would be an enormous draw. With the best will in the world, though we wanted the boys to be as fully involved as possible, there were complicated arrangements to be made requiring expert help and planning. At the first meeting it was readily agreed that the adult management committee had to be involved, and that we would also need to keep in close touch with Tim Brightman, the area secretary, who would be our contact with Frankie. It was clear that the full domestic resources of the school would be required and at Joyce's suggestion Florence Collinson, the matron, was invited to join a small planning committee. She was an ardent fan of Frankie Vaughan and delighted to be asked. The planning group was eventually agreed as Sam Chapman, the adult committee chairman, Vic Wootten, Joyce, Florence and two members of the Boys' Committee in rotation.

Joyce agreed to keep minutes and plans rapidly took shape. There was to be an hour or so in the afternoon when the club would be open and boys could meet Frankie. Starting at six in the evening there would be a dance in the assembly hall. The first hour would be for the boys, and a number of girls from the local secondary school would be invited as partners. The adult dance would start at 7.30pm.

It was hoped that Frankie Vaughan would be present for at least part of each session but Tim Brightman had made it clear that Frankie would be doing the rounds of as many clubs as possible during his two days in Bristol. He had insisted that he wished to see the school in the afternoon and meet boys;

he would also look in during the evening dance but the timing could only be approximate. We had his permission to advertise his coming on our posters and tickets.

Preparations went ahead rapidly and smoothly. Sam Chapman was an old hand at these functions and knew all the right buttons to press. With his influence we got posters and tickets printed free of charge. He helped, through his contacts, with the collection of raffle prizes and a dance band was lined up. When their leader was told they must be ready to accompany Frankie Vaughan if, as was usual, he agreed to sing they were falling over themselves to agree. Joyce and Florence between them co-ordinated the raffle and circulated the staff, friends and local businesses to collect promises to be auctioned. Items such as a box for an evening at the theatre, a meal for four at the local restaurant or a week's holiday in a caravan by the sea would sell easily, but in addition we had all sorts of promises for work or services – three nights babysitting, two days garden clearance and the like.

The big day dawned. The excitement among the ladies on the staff was palpable and they were one and all spruced up for the occasion. A small cavalcade of cars arrived, Tim Brightman, Sam Chapman and Frankie Vaughan in the first car and two further cars with occupants whose functions would no doubt become clear during the day. Even in that day and age, celebrities travelled with an entourage. Frankie duly had his look round the school, accompanied by Bill Hall, and chatted freely to boys. He then set off on the next stage of his lightning tour of clubs in the city.

The first part of the evening dance was, so far as I could see, a total failure. The thirty or so girl guests from the local secondary schools stayed resolutely on one side of the room, while a larger group of boys stayed firmly on the other. The bandleader did his best to encourage participation but the only result of his persuasive powers was to get girls on the floor partnering each other. A 'ladies excuse me' did little better, though Joyce did coax Darrell onto the floor. After half an hour we called time and moved the action from the assembly hall to the clubrooms next door. The dance continued with disco records of the day – much more to the youngsters' tastes.

The adult dance was a success from the first. The bandleader had no difficulty in getting folk on to the floor and when Frankie joined the party the atmosphere was electric. He had already met staff during his afternoon tour and showed a remarkable facility for remembering names. He may have been assisted by his agent who remained close at hand, but it was in any case an impressive performance. We invited him on to the platform to say a few words. He thanked us for allowing him to come, praised the club for the work it was doing and said he hoped everyone would give generously to the raffle and the auction.

"May I give you a song?"

Screams of delight from his audience. He gave us two of his hits, finishing with his trademark theme song. "Give me the moonlight, give me the girls…"

His agent added a selection of his EPs to the raffle prizes, Frankie danced with two or three ladies and then he excused himself as he had two more club engagements during the evening. All in all it was a bravura performance, which added substantially to club funds. We asked Tim Brightman about expenses for the evening but were assured that not only was all Frankie's work for the NABC done without charge but he gave generous financial support as well.

The great and the good

In the summer of 1956 Queen Elizabeth and Prince Philip were to give their official blessing to the Chew Valley Reservoir.

This scheme, already providing water as one of a string of reservoirs supplying Bristol, was now to be officially opened by the highest in the land and we had been invited to send a party of boys, accompanied by staff, to view the proceedings. Dick Adams suggested that either Bill Hall or myself should get this organised; Bill said that he had no particular interest so it was left to me. In due course twenty boys, along with myself, Joyce, two quite excited little girls and Bertie Boast, the Carpenter housemaster, made our way to the lake in the school's Austin Welfarer.

It was a glorious trip on a sunny day through the Somerset countryside. We were directed by police to a pleasant picnic spot by the roadside overlooking the lake. The only other group with us was a similar sized party from the National Nautical School at Portishead, an approved school for senior boys which offered training for those wishing to go to sea. The main welcoming party of city aldermen and assorted dignitaries was well away on the other side of the lake. Perhaps it was thought that our motley group of delinquents would pollute the atmosphere. Whatever the reason we had a wonderful view of the royal party. A couple of motorcycle outriders alerted us and we stood in an orderly line on the grassy road verge.

To the delight of our two little girls, six and two years old respectively, the royal couple stopped to chat to the boys and the Queen accepted a little bunch of wild flowers that Christine had picked for her. I snapped the scene furiously with our ancient, trusty folding camera, using the whole film. Eight photos – what extravagance!

I removed the film, wrapped it up carefully and put it in an envelope ready to post off to Gretispool in Glasgow whence, in due course, we would receive two sets of prints and a free film. What a treasure for the family archives. If only! Two days later we were about to sit down to breakfast when a two-year-old came in with an open reel of film dangling from her hand.

"Look what I've found daddy!"

"Yes sweetheart, it's very interesting." I picked her up and gave her a big hug.

Religious observance and the Methodist tradition

Kingswood had a long and honourable association with John Wesley, the founding father of Methodism. It was here that he had preached to the downtrodden Kingswood miners, and here that he established his first school for local children. The building he erected as a school for the sons of Kingswood miners, a unique establishment in his day, were still in use as workshops for the training school's trade department. The substantial school he eventually built as a boarding school for the sons of his travelling preachers was the building taken over first by Mary Carpenter for her work with delinquent youngsters from Bristol, and eventually as one of the very first schools approved for the treatment of delinquent boys. The first certificate of approval was granted by Lord Palmerston in 1852. Wesley's school had by that time moved on to Bath where it still is.

Wesley's original school was replaced in late Victorian times with a much larger building on the original site. It was clear that the Wesley tradition was valued by the managers and religious observance played a considerable part in the life of the school. Each working day started with a school assembly which included a hymn, a short talk by the head, the deputy or some volunteer from the staff and a concluding prayer. All the boys attended local church services on Sunday morning, generally C of E or Methodist, and there was normally a half-hour service on a Sunday evening at which an address would be given by volunteers from the local community. Surprisingly, these provisions, though compulsory, were not resented in any way by the boys – rather they were welcomed as a change from the usual routine. The main churches attended were remarkably tolerant of the boys and indeed some of them were welcomed to join the senior classes in the Sunday schools.

One of the most useful contacts with the churches was through a link established with a ministerial training college for Methodist ministers, which was situated at Westbury-on-Trym. A team of eight young men from the college were designated as a mission team to visit the training school on a regular basis, at least once a week. They were welcomed into the three houses as voluntary helpers, joining the boys in house activities, playing individuals at board games and participating in team games in the gym or the swimming bath. When the boys' club started they proved invaluable in organising competitions, giving unobtrusive oversight and simply talking to boys as individuals. Active evangelisation was not encouraged but their chosen career as Methodist ministers was known to the whole school and they made no secret of their Christian convictions. Surprisingly perhaps it was youngsters who had had no connections with church or Sunday school before coming to Kingswood who most readily made contact with these young men. When the older boys were no longer able to play in the NABC senior league we welcomed the opportunity given to take a full team to the college to play a friendly match. The Kingswood team was strengthened by the inclusion of two members of staff and the boys had tea and cakes before returning to school. It was a successful and fruitful visit, repeated from time to time.

So far as church attendance was concerned we were richly blessed in the two main churches to which the boys were directed on Sundays. We tried to ensure that anyone who expressed a wish to attend a particular denomination was duly accommodated, but this left a nucleus of around a hundred boys who were noted in their files as either being Anglican or Methodist or as having no particular affiliation. Generally about sixty boys would go to the local C of E church and around forty to the Methodist church. Staff on weekend duty were allocated to escort boys to church. It was done informally and without fuss and it helped that some of the staff who were not on duty would go to church anyway.

Joyce and I, having after our early reservations been warmly received, went as regularly as duties allowed to the Methodist church. There was considerable excitement on one particular Sunday when the minister reminded the congregation of a forthcoming visit by Billy Graham, the American evangelist. It was taking place in London, at the Harringay Arena, but the proceedings were to be rebroadcast to the Methodist Central Hall in Bristol, and the minister invited the congregation to attend. No elaborate television screens, they were unheard of locally at this time, just simple speech transmission. I had no interest myself – I considered Graham's approach far too emotional for my taste – and I was quite sure that the forty or so Kingswood boys in the congregation would certainly have no interest in such matters. You may imagine my shock when the next time I was in full charge of the school I was met by a delegation of six boys. "Please sir, we know you'll be pleased to hear we want to go to hear Billy Graham next Wednesday."

I looked at this motley crew in some astonishment. Three at least were incorrigible rogues with whom we had been able to do little or nothing constructive in the time they had been in the school. Not one of them, so far as I knew, had shown the least interest in things spiritual in their whole lives. What on earth were they playing at? And then it dawned on me. Of course, it was a Wednesday they were talking about, and these were all over-fifteens and therefore in the trade training departments. Wednesday was when they had to spend time doing boring classroom work!

"Tell me more, boys. Convince me. Tell me what you know of Billy Graham?"

It was Stephen who was the spokesman. Perhaps not the best choice to be putting the case to Stanway. Not much more than a year earlier he had achieved fame of a sort with the boys by throwing half a brick at a very new and very apprehensive member of staff. I looked at this unkempt, unprepossessing rogue, doing his best to look innocent and convincing, and in my imagination felt once more the terror of the brick whizzing past my ear and shattering the cupboard door. I had a vision of impending disaster. Their only wish, I was certain, was to have some time off school and a bit of fun at the expense of that very nice group of people from church. And, of course, there were sure to be some attractive young girls about.

"Sorry boys, it's just not on."

They were not really surprised – it had been worth a try.

I went home and told Joyce what had happened. I was quite sure she would be pleased. We were not going ourselves but good friends from the church would be there and it would be unfortunate if our all-too-well-known boys started trouble. I waited to be told how clever I had been to see through their little games. Not a bit of it.

"Who are you to come between these boys and Billy Graham? Where's your Christian faith?"

That was hitting below the belt and I said so, but Joyce could not be assuaged. My arguments about possible trouble, and school responsibility, had no effect.

"I think you should take a risk, in God's name, and let them go!"

No contest. The next day I called the six boys to the office and said that I had had a word with Mrs Stanway and that she said they should be allowed to attend. "You can go boys. Best clothes, no bother or there'll be blood on the moon!"

It would be stretching the truth to say that six boys were permanently changed by their trip to the Central Hall, but all were deeply affected by the experience and were prepared to say so. Three of them steadfastly maintained that they had been 'converted', registered this at the time and were in due course followed up by local churches. All six showed immeasurable improvement in their behaviour in school.

Staff reactions varied. Cynical staff members said that it was a ploy to carry favour with senior staff and accelerate their progress towards licence. Those with a strong Christian faith themselves who had heard the Billy Graham broadcast were both convinced and supportive. My own attitude was ambivalent. As a long-standing lay preacher in the Methodist church, with connections with all the mainstream denominations, I welcomed Billy Graham as a strong force for good while at the same time having reservations about what I saw as an over-enthusiastic approach to evangelisation. It was always clear to me that youngsters who had deeply disturbed family backgrounds could be uniquely vulnerable to any well-meaning folk offering a universal panacea. I did not make any of my doubts public knowledge.

Joyce's attitude was crystal clear – let's judge by results – and there was no doubt that so far as behaviour in the school was concerned, the results were good. All six boys were licensed quite soon and returned to their homes, with careful reference to local churches for follow-up contact. Statistically they all proved to be after-care successes. Of course we could not possibly judge to what extent the Billy Graham experience had contributed to their success but it had clearly done them no harm.

Many years later one of the six sent Joyce and me a book, *My Answer* by Billy Graham. Unusual, in itself, to receive presents from old boys but it was the inscription on the fly leaf which was interesting:

> *With love and grateful thanks to Mrs Stanway.*
> *I hope it may help Mr Stanway to be a better Christian.*

I'm not sure whether it did, but I appreciated the sentiment.

It was automatically assumed by Dick Adams and Bill Hall that, because of my strong association with the local churches as a lay preacher, I would be the one to deal with any problems arising from religious observance. It was not a role with which I was entirely happy. Though I was fully convinced that the attendance of the boys at the local churches was useful, I would have preferred it to be entirely voluntary, but I recognised that this was not practicable if we were to satisfy the Approved School Rules and the wishes of the school managers.

We did our best to cope with the wishes of those boys who, on their own account or through the influence of their parents wished to attend a particular denomination. We had no Jews or Catholics – they had their own approved schools – but if we had boys with Salvation Army, Plymouth Brethren, Pentecostal or indeed any other denominational background, we would get in touch with the appropriate local church. They were always willing to arrange transport to have boys picked up and brought back to school. If from time to time such boys were invited to stay with church members for a meal we raised no objection, though we did make it clear that to comply with regulations we had to run police and Home Office checks.

A useful by-product of these contacts was that we were able to build up a panel of speakers, ordained and otherwise, who were willing to conduct the Sunday evening services that were a regular feature of school life. Bertie Boast, the housemaster in Carpenter House, played the piano for almost all morning assemblies and Sunday services. He could play equally well by ear or from music and had a quite phenomenal memory for tunes. Hum a new tune over to him a couple of times and he would with minimum practice play it with full harmony.

In the written details that we sent out to potential Sunday evening speakers, we made it pretty clear that we did not welcome public appeals for conversion. We pointed out that we had a number of boys who were emotionally or psychiatrically disturbed and who were thus in a particularly vulnerable condition. We did not forbid such appeals altogether but advised that speakers should suggest that any boy who wanted to discuss any matter, spiritual or otherwise, could stay behind after the service for a private conversation with the speaker or any of his or her friends who had come along in support. It was always noticeable that the Pentecostal pastor, who generally took one service a quarter, always had up to a dozen boys stay behind for a chat. Whether it was his eloquence, or the fact that he was always accompanied by three or four members of his congregation, including one or two attractive young ladies, we were never able to decide.

John Blagg was a Byron House boy who stayed behind after one of these services and told the speaker that he was now a Christian. The speaker passed this on to me, with the comment that he was not sure John had much idea what being a Christian meant but would I please follow it up. I duly did so, but John rebuffed my approach, saying he was going to work things out for himself. At his next house meeting he announced to all and sundry that he had decided to be a Christian. This would normally have been an open invitation to some of his mates to test out his faith by mockery and bullying but John was not one who was ever bullied more than once. He was not a big strong boy, but was quite ruthless in dealing with attacks from any boy however big. On the first occasion that he was beaten up he simply awaited his opportunity and, at a point where his main tormentor was entirely off his guard, smashed him on the back of the head with half a brick, laying him out and putting him into hospital for a couple of days recovering from concussion. His subsequent punishment by Bill Hall made no difference to his behaviour and one further similar incident convinced even the most aggressive that he must be left safely alone.

His public confession of Christian belief was received with some cynicism by boys and staff, including me, but no one challenged him or ridiculed him. Apart from those occasional violent episodes, which were not repeated, John was making excellent progress in the school. Not a particularly bright boy, he was a hard worker and proving to be a competent craftsman in the painting and decorating department. One thing we did notice was that he gave up smoking. We put this down to the fact that we had for some time been running a programme to persuade boys to stop smoking on the grounds that it caused ill health, including lung cancer. The school policy on smoking, with which I entirely agreed, aimed at persuasion rather than outright prohibition, which, in the circumstances of the 1950s and early 1960s would have been a waste of effort. There was close control of where boys could smoke – outside or in a rather uncomfortable room in each house and never, on pain of severe punishment, in the bedrooms.

Some six months after John's announcement of his conversion we received a letter from the chief executive of a national cancer charity to tell us that he had received what he described as a very moving letter from John Blagg in our school. John told him in the letter that he had become a Christian, and that this had changed his life. He was no longer going to steal or rob, as he had in the past, and he had also given up smoking. He had saved all the money he would have spent on cigarettes and enclosed a postal order for two pounds five shillings made out to the cancer charity.

The executive ended his letter by saying that he was to be in Bristol in a few days time – would we mind if he visited the school to see John and to thank him personally? Those members of staff, including me, who had viewed John's declaration with considerable cynicism, were suitably chastened. The visit was agreed, and we took the opportunity of getting the visitor to tell the boys, in a specially arranged assembly, something of the background of his charity.

Running away . . .

Like all approved schools Kingswood had occasional problems with boys running away – 'absconding' was the term we used. The police would classify it as 'escaping', not really accurate since the boys were never locked in, the large double gates at the entrance were never closed, let alone locked, and the stone surrounding walls, a relic of a very different past, had broken down or been demolished in many places. Boys could literally walk out at any time, and it was perhaps surprising that, for most of the time, absconding remained a minor problem. It had to be treated seriously, however.

Most runaways were picked up or gave themselves up within twenty-four hours. Providing they had committed no offences outside the school they were returned to their housemaster to be dealt with, normally by a minor loss of privileges. Parents or guardians were informed after a couple of hours or so had elapsed. The real worry was that if the boys were not picked up quickly they would inevitably have to commit some offence in order to be able to eat.

One of the most memorable absconding episodes was when Lee Jones of Wesley House decided to try his luck. An intelligent, but very disturbed, physically immature fourteen-year-old, he seemed quite happy in the house, joined cheerfully in a range of activities and was a keen member of the boys' club. He expressed a wish to join the army, an ambition which was supported by his parents, and eventually he was allowed to join the local army cadet force. His steady progress came to an abrupt stop when his behaviour on his weekly cadet evenings deteriorated so sharply that his cadet officer told him he was no longer welcome in the unit. Not a total veto; he could perhaps come back in a couple of months if the school could give him good reports. Lee was furious, claiming to other boys that he had been unfairly treated and picked on.

"I don't care. I'll get my own back."

A few days later he was missing from afternoon school and duly reported to the police. He was picked up six hours later at Temple Meads station by the railway police in quite ludicrous circumstances. He had made his way to the local cadet depot, broken in and stolen – he would say 'borrowed' for he had no intention of keeping it – an army greatcoat which was at least half a dozen sizes too big, reaching almost to the ground. To complete his bizarre outfit he unhooked a large circular clock from the wall and hung it around his neck concealed inside his greatcoat. He then, to quote the official police report, "proceeded to walk through the main streets of Bristol, stopping from time to time to open the greatcoat to display the clock." Apparently he would ask passers-by whether he had the correct time.

When picked up, without difficulty, by the British Rail police Lee said that he had done it to get back at the army cadets. He was duly collected from the station and returned to his house. He did not abscond again but the account of that one episode duly entered the school folklore. The notoriety he achieved with his fellows gave him new status, and though he was not welcomed back into the cadets he did settle down in school to make steady progress. The greatcoat and clock were returned undamaged!

An absconding of a different calibre was carried through after very careful planning by another Wesley House boy, Eugene Sanson. He was another youngster with military ambitions and one of the very few who joined the army cadets. He fitted in brilliantly and was apparently making excellent all-round progress but, quite unknown to his commanding officer and with no hint of anything amiss in the school, turned out to have been preparing for the most audacious individual absconding in my experience.

Like Lee, he started by breaking into the cadet store, equipping himself with a full selection of kit all carefully chosen to fit, including spare shirts, socks and underwear neatly stowed in army haversacks. Then, with a selection of maps and official stationery, he set off for Scotland. *En route* he obtained accommodation with consummate skill and barefaced cheek at a series of army camps. He began by hitching a ride to Aldershot, where he was fed and accommodated after convincing the guard commander that he was taking part in an initiative exercise. The same ruse provided him with a series of bed and breakfast stopovers at Her Majesty's expense. None of this was known to us at the time. We, and his parents, were very worried that he had simply gone missing.

Having crossed the border, and got as far as Inverness, Eugene returned by a different route to Kingswood, not to resume his career in the school but to spend a few hours sleeping in before moving on to the Southwest. Unfortunately for his further progress there was a police alert on Dartmoor and he was picked up. In due course he was collected by his housemaster from Exeter police station and returned to the school. He had not done any stealing, but there was no doubt some law he had broken – misrepresentation, fraud or whatever – and of course there was the break-in to the army store. The police had no interest in charging him and the school did not press the matter.

Very sensibly Bill Hall, after due discussion with the classifying school, arranged for Eugene to go there rather than come back to Wesley House. He felt, quite rightly, that to other boys he would have become a heroic figure and that this would inevitably have a bad effect on his fellows. In due course he was transferred to a senior school where, according to subsequent reports, he did well.

Another notable flight came after a very settled period in the school, at least so far as absconding was concerned, with no runaways for nearly three months. Even Darrell, the Wesley House boy who had never before gone two months without absconding, was still in school. There was no particular reason that we could see for this general inertia: there were the usual upsets and disciplinary troubles in school but nothing resulting in any absconding. We were not foolish enough to imagine that the problem had gone away, however.

When our quarterly statistics were sent to the Home Office, some mandarin had the bright idea that we were the ones to cope with Jason Culley, a thirteen-year-old from the East End of London. He had been running away every few days from two successive schools, and creating minor mayhem in the school neighbourhoods by petty crime. We could not imagine that we were going to do any better than his previous schools but we had no good reason not to take him. In due course Jason arrived at the school, escorted by a member of staff who expressed considerable relief at passing on the problem. He wished us well and left as soon as possible.

None of our housemasters were keen to accept Jason, who they felt was sure to spoil their excellent records. Bill Hall eventually put him in Carpenter House. The boys there were carefully prepared for his coming by Bertie Boast and were asked both to make a special effort to make him feel welcome and at the same time to watch him and, if possible, prevent him from running away. They took their duties seriously. Two days later Joyce was in our kitchen preparing breakfast when she called out to me in some alarm that half the school was running away. When I joined Joyce and looked up the street, which at that point faced our house, I saw at least twenty boys disappearing out the gate – all in hot pursuit of Jason. In due course they caught him and escorted him back to school.

Our absconding record would quite certainly have gone for a Burton had he stayed with us, but a week or so later there was a home leave period and Jason went off with the rest. For some technical reason concerned with his transfer he did not return. The suggestion was that his parents had objected to him being placed so far from home and had obtained the support of their local MP. Whatever the reason we did not pursue the matter!

. . . *and running for glory*

One of the big sporting events of the year for local boys' clubs was the Bristol to Weston road relay race. Starting from one of the Avon bridges it covered twenty-two miles along the main A370 and finished up on the Weston-Super-Mare sands, where the teams would be met by their enthusiastic supporters and the winners presented with a trophy, generally by the town mayor. It was always splendidly organised, with stewards at each of the changeover points to greet the runners as they came in and give first aid to those who had over-exerted themselves. The stages were of varying distances, with shorter stages for the under-fifteens and three four-mile stages for youngsters up to seventeen. It was invariably run in a very good spirit and the last stage in particular, through the streets of Weston, always attracted enthusiastic spectators.

Our boys, with little love for normal cross-country running, were keen competitors, and we had no difficulty getting them to train. It was a great help that the new housemaster in Byron House was himself a marathon runner and on at least three of the practice runs was prepared to run the whole distance. He was normally given twenty minutes or so start before the first boys set off. Vic Wootten, our boys' club leader, drove the school van with two competing teams and dropped off competitors at each of the change-over points. We always had at least one member of staff to follow the route by car and usually the housemother of Byron House would be there to encourage and cheer on her husband, and to pick him up when he had had enough. He was always overtaken at some point by the youngsters, but not normally until he was just three or four miles from the Weston beach. The boys were deeply impressed with his athletic prowess and it was a considerable help in getting him established in the house.

There would normally be a dozen teams competing in the relay. The highest position we achieved was third, on two separate occasions. On each we were in the lead up to the last long stage through Weston but the two teams who overtook us, quite comfortably in the end, had older and very proficient runners for the last stage.

After the reception for all the teams on the sands we were given the option of moving on to the local secondary school for showers and a change of clothes, and there was invariably a relaxed and happy gathering of competitors. We then dipped into club funds to get take-away fish and chips for all the competitors and the reserves.

For reasons which were never made quite clear the race ceased to be held after a few years. It was getting increasingly difficult in terms of road traffic. I did hear that the police, originally very supportive and helpful, were laying down ever more stringent conditions for their co-operation. One suggestion – that the race could be run in late spring or summer and start at 6am – was turned down flat.

Sex offenders

There was a period in the mid fifties when we were saddled – or blessed! – with all juvenile sex offenders who were committed to the approved school system from the whole of the region from Birmingham to Land's End. So far as the magistrates and the classifying school were concerned there were good reasons for this since, at the time, we were the only approved school in the country which had resident clinical psychological or psychiatric help. There was an almost universal assumption that any fourteen-to sixteen-year-old who committed a serious sexual offence must, *per se*, be in need of psychiatric attention, and this recommendation would be attached to the court report and sent with the boy to the classifying school. There were in fact very few cases anyway and those we did get varied considerably in the seriousness of the offence. Of perhaps five cases a year, a typical breakdown would be two instances of indecent exposure (commonly known as 'flashers'), two indecent assaults and perhaps one serious rape.

If we were to keep our good reputation in the community, which had been carefully nurtured over the years, the first essential for us was to prevent any incidents in the locality. We began by preserving anonymity, a much easier task in the 1950s and 1960s than it would be today. I cannot remember any press coverage of the cases referred to us. There were no articles even hinting at any difficulties we might encounter and for this we were profoundly grateful. We emphasised to staff that for all our boys, but particularly for this group, there must be no gossip, not even in the family.

Having the benefit of being on the same site as the classifying school, though quite separate, was a great advantage to us in dealing with these sex offenders. All the preliminary psychiatric assessment was done before the offenders were sent down to us and invariably John Briers, our psychologist, would have prior access to the papers and could interview the boys for himself if he so wished. What we particularly needed was a risk assessment.

Those regarded as presenting minimal risk were dealt with in a routine manner: a careful watch as with all new boys but the normal classroom or department training. Perhaps we were fortunate – though I would prefer to think that it was the skilled assessment of our psychiatrist and psychologist – but with only one exception, which I will describe later, we did not have any serious incidents of a sexual nature outside the school. I emphasise 'serious' as, like all approved schools, we would have the occasional complaint from some parent in the neighbourhood saying that they did not fancy their whiter-than-white daughter being chatted up or even kissed by one of our boys at youth club, or church social or whatever. In practice the girls were almost invariably more sexually mature than our boys and when we investigated they were usually the ones who had taken the initiative. In the interests of good community relationships we always investigated, but generally there was nothing to get too concerned about and the boys involved were referred to their housemaster for a fatherly chat.

There were one or two only who were deemed a serious risk, and for these the treatment was clear. They all accepted – or at least could not deny – that they had committed or attempted a very serious assault and that their impulses and sex drive were out of control. They were therefore referred to the psychologist for what amounted to an intensive course of therapy. Difficulties arose when a boy, while accepting that he had a problem which could be beyond his control, refused to co-operate in his therapy, but the answer was simple enough. He would be prescribed a course of treatment with some drug which effectively reduced his sex drive to a safe level – Stilboestrol or the like. Such treatment was established as routine and it worked.

Providing we had the co-operation of parents and after-care agents so that treatment, of whatever sort, could be carried on at home, these youngsters were normally licensed after a year or fifteen months. Since they were generally around sixteen when committed, much older than our normal admission ages, this meant that if they committed any further offence, they could be charged as an adult. This was explained to them and proved a powerful deterrent. We did not fool ourselves that we had effected any serious rehabilitation with these sad young men but we had at least kept them out of circulation for a period and given useful guidance for future treatment, in units with more staff and closer supervision than was possible for us.

The one incident outside the school that could have had repercussions concerned Daniel, a lanky, ill-coordinated sixteen-year-old who had been committed for several offences of indecent exposure. Unlike most cases of 'flashing' he was foolish enough to expose himself to middle-aged or older ladies whom he knew, so inevitably he would always be caught. There were no doubt more incidents than those with which he was charged, because a number of the victims were so sorry for Daniel's widowed mother that apart from telling her what had happened so that she could deal with Daniel they took no further action. One hefty matron took unilateral action and gave him a hearty whack with her stick. Inevitably, in the end, Daniel's behaviour came to the notice of the police and resulted in an Approved School Order, with a recommendation for psychiatric treatment.

Daniel was assessed as low risk and slotted into school routine with no problems. Two home leaves passed without incident and things seemed set fair for early licence. One of the ways we were hoping to help him was to enable him to have normal access to some older, responsible young ladies and to achieve this end we were fortunate to have two postgraduate students from Bristol University who visited the school regularly to give voluntary help in the youth club. One of the projects they were involved with was to help prepare a Christmas show: part pantomime, part concert.

That particular year the plans were a bit more ambitious than usual and we decided to invite various organisations – pensioners' clubs, groups from the local churches and some of our neighbours – to enjoy an evening's entertainment. Our two postgraduates were enthusiastically preparing the pantomime bits of the show. They wrote the dialogue, enlisted expert help from their own drama group in creating costumes, and were quite prepared to take part themselves. As the date for the grand opening drew near, rehearsals became more frenetic. To move things along we allowed Daniel and two others who were performing with him to go down to the university for a costume fitting. All went well, the costumes were duly fitted as planned and then the three boys were told to go to the dressing room to change into their school clothes. It was at that point that Daniel chose to expose himself to the two young ladies. Singularly foolish, as it was bound to be reported.

The two girls were quite prepared to accept an apology from Daniel, delivered in grovelling fashion, but Bill Hall very properly vetoed any further participation by Daniel in the production, which went ahead without him. However, this temporary set-back to Daniel's behaviour did not have any serious repercussions. He was licensed quite soon and, with careful supervision from his after-care agent, a woman probation officer, settled down to make steady progress.

Violent behaviour

The following two case histories were not at all unusual for us. They are included to give an idea of problems we faced in getting outside help for our youngsters, from the courts or from specialist institutions.

Martin Jensen was an unprepossessing youth who had very little going for him at home, or indeed in life, with a long history of petty crime and many problems at his day schools. He had just turned fifteen when he came to us and was illiterate, innumerate and anti-authority. His parents had firmly rejected him and his one hope in the family, a married older sister who was the only relative to stay in regular contact, was understandably reluctant to risk the stability of her own family by offering him a permanent home. The best option we could come up with for his future was to place him near enough to his sister to enable some contact.

In the school he was placed in the stonemasonry department and we arranged some extra tuition in basic subjects in the schoolroom. Unfortunately his clumsiness at work did not endear him to his fellows and Norman Oxley, his instructor, had to intervene regularly to settle squabbles. Generally minor, but there was an alarming escalation on once occasion when Martin reacted to some insignificant teasing by hitting his mate on the hand with a stonemason's lump hammer and breaking two fingers. Norman was escorting him over to the office for Bill Hall to deal with when Martin drew a concealed flick knife and stabbed the instructor in the lower abdomen. It was pure chance that it was not a serious wound, but Bill Hall quite properly judged that it should not be dealt with on a school basis. The police were informed and Martin was immediately arrested and charged with grievous bodily harm.

After a night in a police cell he was to appear in the local juvenile court, where we confidently expected him to be remanded in custody for the preparation of reports. We assumed that with his record, and the gravity of the offence, he would be sent on for Borstal training. Norman's bloodstained underwear was retained by the police as evidence, to be produced for the magistrates if necessary, and Martin's housemaster went to court to attend what we assumed would be a purely formal appearance. Unfortunately for us, and to our embarrassment since we had not produced any proper reports, assuming they could come at a later date, the magistrates paid no attention to our concerns and simply returned the boy to the school.

Out of consideration for Norman and the other boys on the stonemasonry department, we moved Martin to the gardening department but his behaviour deteriorated sharply. There was no doubt that the reaction of the other boys to his return contributed to his difficulties. Norman Oxley was a popular member of staff and Martin was twice attacked by boys in reprisal. He was eventually, after a good deal of discussion, returned to the classifying school for re-assessment. We expected that he would

211

in due course be returned to us but he viciously attacked another boy for no apparent reason and was eventually, after a good deal of further violence, admitted to secure mental hospital accommodation on an indefinite basis.

A more positive outcome, though surprising to all concerned, was in the case of Nigel Deere. Like all approved schools we were used to dealing with boys with a history of violence before coming to us but Nigel was something special. Rejected by his parents and two sets of foster parents, he had also been tried out in two different approved schools. In each of these he had made serious assaults on members of staff. The one subject he was good at and enjoyed was woodwork but it was in the woodwork shop that, after just some minor irritation, he attacked first of all another boy quite viciously and then his teacher, who was seriously wounded with a Stanley knife when he attempted to intervene. After two similar episodes he was returned to the classifying school for re-allocation. When a psychiatric assessment stated that he had 'a florid psychosis' it was almost inevitable that he would be sent to us to be treated by John Briers, our resident clinical psychologist.

The new report from the classifying school made bleak reading, but was quite clear on one point – he should not be put on the woodwork department where he would have immediate access to dangerously sharp tools. Where could he be placed? We tried him for a few days in the stonemasonry department and he created mayhem. His painting and decorating career lasted a little longer, but finished when he pushed one of his fellows off a stepladder and then hit him with a tin of paint. In the end he was given a desk in the corridor outside the head's office and allocated enough worksheets to keep him busy for a few days. We recognised that this could only be a very temporary arrangement while arrangements were being made for more positive treatment elsewhere. We had been given details of a newly established facility in Somerset providing treatment to adolescent boys with psychiatric problems. It could take a maximum of thirty youngsters, was generously staffed and had full mental health facilities. It sounded ideal for Nigel, and John Briers duly completed all the necessary paperwork supported by further psychiatric reports.

We were delighted when word came back quickly that Nigel could be accepted as a voluntary patient. John Briers gave him the news, and secured his agreement to go. His housemother packed his gear and we sent him off with our good wishes and no little relief, along with John and one of our two social workers who was keen to have a look at this splendid new facility.

They came back full of enthusiasm. A new building, splendidly equipped, not yet fully staffed but already with three nursing shifts to give twenty-four-hour coverage. Staffing levels we could only dream about! John wrote optimistic summaries in the file and we turned thankfully to other matters. I was particularly relieved because Bill Hall was about to leave for a fortnight's holiday, leaving me in charge, and I was no keener than anyone else to confront a violent fifteen-year-old wielding a chisel or a Stanley knife – or even a can of paint.

A peaceful weekend was cut short at ten o'clock on Sunday evening by a telephone call from Somerset. It was the sister in charge of the special unit.

"I'm very sorry, but you'll have to come and collect Nigel, he's rampaging round the unit and we can't control him."

I was thunderstruck. How was it to be supposed that we could do what a much more generously staffed unit could not achieve? I argued the point vigorously, pointing out that they had had the boy for less than forty-eight hours and that they had agreed with us that he needed their facilities. All to no avail. Nigel was a voluntary admission, he did not wish to stay with them and under the conditions of acceptance we had to take him back. I reluctantly agreed that we would collect him the next day.

"No, he must be collected at once. He's absolutely out of control."

What could we do? Why had this happened when Bill Hall was away? My heart sank, I could see no way forward. I managed at least to defer the problem for a few hours by giving my approval for Nigel to be taken into police custody overnight while we made arrangements to have him collected the next day. John Briers was not available so we arranged for Charlie Betteridge, his housemaster, to collect him. After a good deal of thought, and with a half-formed treatment plan in mind, I arranged for Theo Griffiths to take over the carpentry department for the day so that Howard Poolman, the regular woodwork instructor, could accompany Charlie. I suggested that during the journey Howard just might be able to get Nigel to open up about his hopes and ambitions, and in particular about his love of woodwork. No great expectations but we were desperate.

In the event the contact with Howard succeeded better than we had dared to hope. It helped that Howard had not read the file and approached the youngster in a free and easy way. When they returned to school I sat Nigel and his two escorts down in my office for a chat. I kicked off by telling him that he had made a total mess of things. "What on earth are we going to do with you now? You've wasted every chance you've been given for years."

That was the point at which Howard jumped in. "I'd like him to be given a chance in the woodwork shop."

I was guilt stricken. I knew that, without putting it into words, this was what I had hoped, but what about his previous record? What about the very firm recommendations from the classifying school? What about the safety of other boys? At the same time, what possible alternative did we have?

"What do you want Nigel?"

"Please, sir, I want to be with Mr Poolman."

My mind was made up immediately: we were going to give him the chance. But before agreeing I played the devil's advocate and put forward powerful arguments why he should not go to the woodwork shop. I detailed some of the violence in the past, including attacks on teachers. In the end I sent him back to his house to get a meal and a shower, and said that we'd think about it and let him know.

Howard and I then had a full and frank discussion. I got him to read the file and, as I had expected, it did not put him off at all. In fact it turned out that the conversation they had had on the way back to school had been very informative and that Nigel had been open and frank with Howard about his previous violence. It occurred to me, not for the first time, that Howard, short and physically pretty insignificant, had the inestimable gift of inspiring respect from the youngsters he dealt with. Of course it was helped by the fact that he was a consummate craftsman, that he loved his work and could impart his skills to others, but the real secret was that he had a deep and genuine love for the damaged youngsters with whom he dealt. His final summing up was simple: "He deserves a new start and I'd like to give it a go."

I kept an anxious eye on Nigel for the next couple of weeks while Bill Hall was away. I could see no alternative to the decisions we had taken, but the responsibility for the safety of staff and boys was on my shoulders and it was all too easy to imagine the furore if there were a further serious assault by this unpredictable youngster.

That our treatment of Nigel was, in the end, brilliantly success-ful – in that he became an upstanding member of society and a first-rate carpentry craftsman – was due primarily to a dedicated instructor who saw boys not as problems but as opportunities. However, there was another factor in the rehabilitative process which I only discovered weeks later when I had a follow-up conversation with Nigel. The forty-eight hours or so he had spent in the special unit had been a quite horrifying experience for him. He put it succinctly: "They were a bunch of nutters – if I'd been there a week I'd have been barmy as well."

When I wrote to the unit thanking the staff for their willingness to help and expressing regret for Nigel's intransigence I did not mention his summing up of his stay!

Months later, when Nigel was happily settled and doing well in the carpentry department, we discussed Nigel's case at a senior staff meeting. John Briers summed up, saying that the placement, short as it was, was a success because it happened to come at exactly the right moment in Nigel's psychiatric development. "He saw a vision of Bedlam, a picture of his possible future which scared him."

Staying in touch

It was an important aspect of the work at Kingswood, and indeed at all approved schools, to keep a check on boys who had been licensed. There was a statutory duty to follow up all boys for a total of six years from the date they were committed or until they reached the age of nineteen, whichever date came first. Each had an after-care agency appointed as soon as possible after they entered the school. If there was already an agency working with the boy or the family – a children's officer or probation officer – the contact was continued unless there were good reasons to the contrary. It was always a matter for discussion with the agency concerned. Changes would be made if, for instance, the relationship between agent and family had broken down. Sometimes the officer concerned would simply suggest that it might be a good idea to try someone new in view of the boy's changed circumstances.

Once an agency was agreed and a named officer appointed, he or she would be the main contact with the family. Home visits by staff were always to be agreed in advance with the after-care agent – that at least was the theory. Case conferences on boys were arranged well in advance and the after-care agent invited to attend. Generally speaking these arrangements worked very well, and they were crucially important as boys approached the time they were to be licensed. The after-care agent played a vital role in getting the boy re-established at home or, if home contact had completely broken down, in lodgings and in helping the youngster to adjust to work or, in a few cases, day school.

The average length of stay for a boy at Kingswood in my time was around fifteen months. The minimum period was six months – a special Home Office dispensation was needed for a boy to be licensed before this – and the maximum was the three years for which he had been committed. After licence he could be recalled to the school at any time during this first three-year period. In practice this was only done after careful consultation with the family, the after-care agent, and the boy concerned. Sometimes, when things were going badly wrong at home or work, a boy would himself ask to be allowed to return, but more often it was a step taken at the after-care agent's initial request in order to avoid impending breakdown.

After the first three-year period was up supervision continued for a maximum of a further three years or until the nineteenth birthday. During this period the young man could be recalled for up to three months in school. This was a rare occurrence, carried out only with the agreement of the youngster himself.

It was not to be encouraged, as almost invariably it was looked for when someone was failing to adjust at home or in lodgings; the school then became a place where he could escape from the demands of life rather than face up to them.

With up to eighty boys being licensed each year there was always a steady stream of reports coming in. Housemasters were responsible for filing these and for keeping a careful check on what was happening at home. It was important to anticipate trouble rather than mop it up after it had happened. Signs were generally pretty clear – loss of job, arguments at home, breakdown of lodgings – but the precipitating factor might also be simply an impression picked up by an experienced social worker. At such times a home visit by the housemaster or school social worker, in co-operation with the after-care agent, could often avoid trouble. Such after-care work was just as important, if not more so, than the work in school.

As well as the records kept by the houses in boys' individual files there was a central, visual record kept in the head's office. This consisted of a separate sheet of drawing paper for each licensing year, all pinned on a large notice board,. Each sheet had an outline human figure with a name beneath it for every boy licensed in the year. Thus when I started at Kingswood there were sheets on the board dating from 1950 to 1956. The 1950 chart would soon be completed and removed, while the 1956 chart consisted of rows of blank outlines, awaiting names as boys came up for licence.

All the sheets with the exception of the most recent had blotches of red ink scattered around the charts. These were simple visual indications of trouble that the boys had got into after leaving the school. Any court appearance or police involvement, even for minor traffic offences, would result in part of the figure being filled in red. I can't at this distance recall the full code

– it started with an arm for a minor traffic offence and moved up to a completely red figure for a further custodial sentence. Any red on any figure meant that the youngster in question was recorded as a failure. It was, of course, only a rough and ready measure of success or failure, but it had the merit of simplicity and clarity. We might feel that it was grossly unfair to record a seventeen-year-old as a failure because he had broken the speed limit on his motorcycle while travelling to a job at which he was doing very well and through which he was contributing to society and his family, but this was the official system which was clearly understood by all concerned. In practice we could always take into account the full circumstances, and if a youngster who had been convicted of minor traffic offences requested a reference there would be no question of our stigmatising him as a failure notwithstanding that he might appear as such on the official record.

In spite of their rough and ready nature these charts gave a good indication of performance. Things balanced out on the whole because there were also individuals who, though technically squeaky clean on our charts because they had no involvement with the police, could only be regarded as failures. Some might have committed offences not yet discovered; one eighteen-year-old might be living with a girlfriend whom he was ill treating or with an infant he was failing to support; another might have a quite appalling work record in spite of the best efforts of his after-care agent. Such youngsters had no red patches on their licence figure but in our eyes they could hardly be classed as successes.

I was asked at one stage after I became club leader to compare our own assessment of success or failure with the official record. This meant that some figures with scattered red patches were unofficially reclassified as successes, on the basis that they were living useful, constructive lives, while others for reasons I have already indicated were unofficially designated as failures. I was interested to find that the balance stayed very much the same. In those early years the success rate stayed pretty steady at somewhere between sixty and seventy per cent. It was not until the 1960s that this impressive success rate began to plummet. The reasons for the decline were complex, but all approved schools suffered the same sort of falling off, and certainly Kingswood was by no means the worst.

Each year there would be one or two boys who, for various reasons, could not be placed back in their home area after licensing. Perhaps their families had become completely shattered, or perhaps the boy had developed such an affinity with the district that he wished to stay. We discouraged such placements as far as we were able. From our point of view it added to staff pressures, since the boys placed locally almost inevitably kept up direct connections with the school and in some cases took up a great deal of staff time.

Over the years the school had managed to find an excellent group of local landladies who were prepared to take some of our most difficult youngsters and give them a new start. There were some advantages from their point of view – lodging payments, rather more than the usual rates, were guaranteed by the school. The boys were expected to pay a fair share from their wages but we always ensured, through the welfare officer attached to the school who was after-care agent for all these boys, that they had sufficient pocket money. The extra allowances were billed to the local authorities from where the boys had been committed and were paid without question. A good bargain from the authority's point of view as it was easier and cheaper for them than finding lodgings in their area and finding staff to give the necessary supervision.

Work was one problem that we always managed to settle., as the local councils always seemed to be short of labour. The bus company was favoured by some youngsters, especially those with ambitions to be drivers. They could start off as cleaners on the night shift – attractive because it carried extra wages – and those who were good with money and giving change were readily taken on as conductors, still employed in those days on all local bus routes.

We slipped up with Frank, an intelligent but incorrigibly dishonest youngster from rural Somerset. He was a handsome, well set-up seventeen-year-old by the time he was licensed, but with a record of petty pilfering and shoplifting which stretched back over the years. Most of his defalcations had been in his small home village and the children's officer responsible for the family was quite certain that for Frank to return there would lead to early disaster. Frank agreed cheerfully with this assessment, although he said that he loved his widowed mother and wished to keep contact with her. To this end employment with the bus company seemed a good option since he would have concession fares on country bus services and could visit his mother quite regularly at low cost. Apart from his feelings for his mother Frank much preferred to be in Bristol, describing his home village as "dead from the neck up". Not a particularly apt metaphor but we could see what he meant, and so from all points of view local lodgings seemed a good option. We arranged an interview for him at the nearest bus depot and in due course he informed us that they were considering his appointment and would be contacting the school for a reference.

A letter duly arrived in the school and I remember reading Bill Hall's reply and reference with wry amusement – it was a minor masterpiece. There were so many good things he could say about Frank's intelligence, his capacity for hard work on the department, his above average academic attainment and his pleasant appearance and personality. He could not, however, ignore his repeated dishonesties, and though he did not go into detail about these there was a very clear implication that he should not be trusted with handling money. Sadly the advice was not taken and Frank came back, quite delighted, to tell us he had been taken on as a bus conductor. Bill Hall took the reasonable view that the company had been warned and we waited with baited breath for disaster.

A month went by without anything happening on his route. We had regular reports from staff because he was allocated to the route crossing right across Bristol and finishing in Kingswood. Some of the staff had been on his bus and were able to say that he had given them first class and cheerful service and that he got on well with all the passengers. We began to breathe more freely but it was too good to last – the first hint of trouble was when his conductor's bag, with whatever money he had taken in the day, was stolen. Quite possible, of course, since the story was that he had left it on a seat in a transport café at the Kingswood end of his run where they had a half hour break. Very careless of course, but he managed, with his undoubted charm, to convince his boss to give him another chance. Unfortunately the same thing happened a fortnight or so later and this time he was summarily dismissed. With his now disastrous work record we were going to have great difficulty finding him another job and just to add to his and our difficulties his landlady decided that, charming as he was, she had had quite enough of his lies and petty thieving from the various little boxes in which she deposited small amounts of money for gas, electricity rates and the like.

The three years of Frank's original committal were well past but there were still a few months of his supervision left and we took him back into school, with his ready agreement, while we made a final attempt to get him sorted. His housemaster gave him a good dressing down and insisted that if we were to be able to help we had to know the full story of what had happened to the money. It was quite simple. There was a bookmaker's office near to the bus terminus – not, at that time, a betting shop with chairs and a television but bets could be placed – and it was there that the bus money had disappeared.

Frank left Kingswood finally at the point where we had run out of options and could no longer keep him in school. He returned to his home village in Somerset to settle in with his long-suffering, patient mother. When the full term of his supervision finished he had, astonishingly, not had any court appearances or convictions since being licensed, so his figure on the after-care chart remained a pristine white.

We did see him again a few years later when he came back to school in a car, in company with an attractive young lady and a baby. He introduced us to them, with some pride, as his fiancée and family and invited us to wish him well as he was shortly to be married. We were assured, by both of the happy couple, that he was now properly settled, living in a flat in Bridgwater, and that he had a job in a local factory. I would like to think that the school played some part in the successful outcome to Frank's story but it was clear that the main credit was due to an intelligent and strong-minded young woman.

Another old boy whose success was due to another such was Tim Harman. He was an overweight, tall, uncouth, somewhat dull lad with little going for him either in school or at home. His father had deserted the family when Tim was an infant and from then until he first came into the approved school system at the age of ten he had had a succession of 'uncles' in the home, none of whom had treated him kindly. By the time he came to us at the age of thirteen he had already been in two different approved schools and a succession of foster homes after his own home had been deemed totally unsuitable. To add to his other multifarious problems he was mildly epileptic, and although this was under good control by drugs it would have serious consequences for employment. It would certainly rule out work as a heavy lorry driver, which seemed to be his only ambition.

We placed him in Carpenter House, where he was at least tolerated by other boys though their general opinion was that he was a 'nutter'. As though he had to prove them right he began to display various bizarre mannerisms culminating in a bout of self-harm. Two of his dormitory companions – one could not call them friends – were sufficiently concerned for his welfare to see Joyce urgently to tell her that Tim had swallowed half a dozen drawing pins and a small pen knife. We couldn't take chances and sent him at once to the local hospital, where X-rays revealed that there was indeed an incongruous collection of potentially dangerous objects in his stomach. He was, of course, kept in and fortunately the objects were cleared by natural means without the need for surgery.

When Tim's licensing opportunity came up there seemed little point in keeping him further in school. His probation officer had found him decent lodgings and he was duly licensed and found work as a labourer with a building firm. To our surprise the report we received after twelve months indicated that by then he had formed relationships with an attractive young woman and moved in with her. What she could see in him was beyond our understanding but in due course they were married, settled down in a council flat and we had no further responsibility to follow up his progress.

It was several years later that we saw him again. He was driving a heavy lorry, his wife was in the cab with him nursing a bonny looking daughter and there was a pushchair folded up beside them. He had finally achieved his ambition, though how he had gained his licence given his medical history of epilepsy we could not imagine. He assured Joyce, who was the one to whom he really wanted to show off his family, that he had not had an epileptic attack for more than two years.

Some time had elapsed after their departure before Joyce got round to telling me the full story of their marriage, family, work and so on. What about Tim's violent temper and bizarre behaviour, I asked.

"Not a problem," said Joyce.

"Oh come on, he's six foot, bad tempered and violent and she's not much more than five foot. She must have had some bad times, has he never hit her?"

"Oh yes," said Joyce, and with a twinkle in her eye recounted the full conversation with Tim and his wife.

"He gave me a black eye once when his dinner wasn't ready in time," confided the young woman cheerfully.

"What did you do?"

"I waited until he'd calmed down and then told him, 'Tim Harman, you sleep like a log. If ever you hit me or Tracey again I shall wait until you are fast asleep, pull the clothes back, take the sharpest kitchen knife I've got and cut your balls off!'"

"And she meant it," added Tim.

"And he's never hit me, or Tracey, again."

Not recommended as family therapy but certainly effective.

From brickbats to bouquets

Towards the end of the period covered by this book we were provided with perhaps the most fitting summary of the progress we had been able to make with some of the youngsters in our care. Four boys were to be licensed the following day, and two of them were among the motley crew whom Joyce had persuaded me to allow to visit the Methodist Central Hall to hear Billy Graham. It was these two who knocked at our door just after the evening house meeting. To my surprise they held out two bunches of flowers, no doubt pinched from the school gardens.

"What a nice surprise boys! Are they for me?"

I was soon disabused. "Can we see Mrs S?"

The subsequent conversation as reported by Joyce was quite straightforward.

"We've brought you some flowers, Miss."

"Just a minute, Stephen, aren't you the one who welcomed Mr Stanway with a brick on his first Wednesday in the school?"

"Yes, Miss, I shouldn't have done it. He's not such a bad sort."

"Well shouldn't you tell him that yourself, and give him the flowers?"

"Oh no, we wouldn't do that."

Hardly the most ringing endorsement! Even so, this little deputation provided some indication of the changed esteem in which Joyce and I were held after our first tumultuous years at Kingswood. It was the culmination of what had been, at times, a challenging journey from brickbats to bouquets.

POSTSCRIPT

Lessons learned

Looking back over the years to my early professional life has been both a cathartic and a humbling experience. Cathartic because my first disastrous encounters in Byron House have been brought sharply into focus and I can now see them as part of my essential development professionally. The demons have been exorcised! Humbling because reflecting on how many times I came near to professional disaster I realise how much I owed to the support of colleagues and, above all, to the steadfast encouragement of Joyce. If she had ever faltered on those occasions when I crept home from house duty feeling like a wrung out dish-rag, I would have gone under.

When things settled down for me at Kingswood, and I had the leisure to do some further studies and to re-examine my basic philosophies of education, I realised the depths of my initial ignorance. I was not alone in this respect. I am quite sure that at Kingswood we had the full range of psychological, behavioural and educational problems which today would quite properly be given appropriate labels and treatment geared to the boys' individual needs. We had youngsters who would be classed as suffering from alexia, dyslexia, autism, attention deficit disorder and the like. In the 1950s these words were never mentioned in the reports we received. Instead, previous school reports used words like 'lazy', 'careless', 'slap-dash', 'anti-authority' and the like.

If we could not put proper names to the disorders, what we did do was to recognise needs and to establish programmes to deal with the shortcomings. Boys severely retarded in reading were put into the reception class into the care of Theo Griffiths. We knew that success in reading was the absolute pre-requisite for all schoolroom progress. This was at a time when 'look and say' was the accepted method of teaching reading: fine for the bright and the educationally committed but disastrous for the dyslexics and the anti-school types with a sad history of previous failure. Theo had a battery of teaching methods and reading schemes brought with him from his previous ESN school, but his emphasis was on phonics. Boys flourished under his tuition, dyslexics and the difficult alike!

So far as treatment regimes in the houses were concerned I was as ignorant about different treatment methods as I was about dyslexia and the like. I had read a few books by some of the pioneers in the treatment of maladjustment, but had dismissed them as not applicable to an approved school subject to the 1933 Home Office Rules. We had three houses which were different in their approach. Carpenter House had Mr and Mrs Boast as housemaster and housemother. Well established, with a team which had been stable for years, the house ran like clockwork. The regular house meetings were useful in allowing boys to express their views, but it was always quite clear that in the end the housemaster's viewpoint would prevail. It was a benevolent autocracy, useful for those youngsters who needed a firm but accepting regime but not advisable for those boys who needed freedom of expression.

Wesley House was the particular concern of John Briers, our clinical psychologist. It was regarded by some staff not directly involved in the house, those who covered house duties on rare occasions, as a chaotic mess. It was, however, ideal for the very disturbed youngsters who needed careful and regular casework. We were fortunate to have Charlie Betteridge and his wife, Olga, as house staff. They were accepting of deviance, dealt lovingly with boys in dire need and were open to new ideas. Their broadmindedness enabled the house to move steadily towards the ideal John Briers was working towards of a full therapeutic approach in an approved school. This was finally achieved in 1964 after I had been appointed headmaster, when I collaborated with John Briers to produce a memorandum for the development of a therapeutic community within the training school. This was well into the future during the time covered in this book, but the necessary casework background was already in place, developing apace and offering the classifying school a valued resource for dealing with boys with acute psychiatric problems.

Byron House, once Phillip and his henchmen had moved on, was developing a very distinct approach of its own. The new houseparents were keen, dedicated and caring, but with no previous experience of work with children other than in limited voluntary capacities. That was the negative side; the positive was that they, and John Inkley who had taken my place as deputy housemaster, were receptive to new ideas. In particular they accepted the concept of shared responsibility which had been shown to work well in the boys' club.

I write of the various treatment systems, 'benevolent autocracy', 'therapeutic community' and 'shared responsibility', as though they were familiar to me, but in the 1950s they were an unknown country. Like a number of other approved schools at the time we were, however, developing rapidly to meet the differing needs of delinquent youth in society. It was, in one sense, fortunate that we were not wedded to any one particular approach but were ever ready to experiment and change according to circumstances and need. Each system has its advantages and disadvantages, and must be flexible enough to cope with individual idiosyncrasies.

Having read my chapters on the youth club and my appointment as deputy head, you will have gathered that I lean towards a regime of shared responsibility, but there are obvious limitations. There are few schools, day or boarding, which do not run to some extent on the basis of shared responsibility, but there is a world of difference between those schools which throw the children a few crumbs from the decision-making table and those which run a properly organised and structured system. We recognised from the start at Kingswood, both in the youth club and in Byron House, that shared responsibility did not mean self-government and that all participants in the process would have laid down limits to their spheres of action. Within these limits the various committees or the whole community as a body should have absolute power; outside them the responsibility of whoever was appropriate would be recognised.

One danger in such a system is that dominant personalities, either staff or boys, can monopolise the decision-making process. If the adults, by virtue of their greater experience, regularly exercise undue control, meetings become a sham and the children lose interest. If, on the other hand, the adults taking part in the meeting are prepared to divest themselves of authority and allow the decisions, within the limits laid down, to go against them there is an immediate bonus in effectiveness and participation. When there is a division of opinion among the adults and a genuine debate being carried on, the children not only gain useful insights into the democratic processes but gain in self-confidence as it becomes increasingly obvious that their own opinions have worth.

In house and school meetings at Kingswood we made it clear that matters under discussion fell into three groups: those where the meeting would take full responsibility and for which the decision would be binding, each member having one vote; those where full discussion was welcomed and the meeting could express its opinions, which would be taken into account but would not be binding; and those where decisions must be taken outside the meeting and where any lengthy discussion would be a waste of time.

In practice, Byron House adopted the new ideas with enthusiasm. Joyce was invited to attend meetings whenever her duties allowed and I was invited very occasionally when there was an item relating to the youth club coming up. It was not appropriate for me to attend regularly but there was one very useful meeting I remember when Joyce and I took diametrically opposing views. I mustered only two supporters for my viewpoint and conceded defeat as gracefully as possible. A small matter for me but a powerful fillip to the status of the house meeting!

Apart from the pleasure I have had in writing this book I would like to think that it might serve some purpose in dealing with delinquent youth today. It would be naïve and foolish to imagine that we can resurrect the approved school system from its ashes. Society has changed and, though the 'flog 'em and hang 'em' brigade might disagree, we would not now accept any system where there was the ultimate sanction of a boy being beaten with an approved Home Office cane. Nevertheless there is a continuing acute problem with disaffected and delinquent youth which must be tackled at some stage in the not too distant future. The present sanctions – ASBOs, care orders, probation, orders against parents – all have a place but clearly only work with some, perhaps a minority of youngsters. It is easy to see that we need something different. The problem will get worse, I suspect, as the gap between rich and poor gets wider, and the moral constraints which used to operate throughout society continue to weaken. Whatever further action is eventually needed it will only come about if there is agreement across the political spectrum. One could envisage a committee with a brief to look at what succeeded in the past, to examine a variety of suggestions for the future and to come up with some positive suggestions.

I would be very surprised if some such committee did not come up with suggestions for a range of residential provision with varying degrees of security, including an extension of present provision of secure accommodation for youngsters.

This book is a memoir of what happened to me during my early traumatic months at Kingswood and it would be presumptuous, and beyond its scope, for me to go into detail about what I would envisage as suitable institutions and programmes for dealing with today's increasingly disaffected youth. It would, however, be very strange if, after thirty years working at the sharp end and progressing from near despair and dismal failure to running schools which, by independent assessment, were judged successful institutions, I did not have some positive ideas. When the committee I have envisaged does eventually meet and, as is usual in such cases, invites representations from the public I shall be happy to put forward detailed suggestions covering a range of options. One thing of which I am quite certain is that there is no one size which fits all.

Acknowledgements

I would not wish to finish this book without acknowledging my debts to the many folk who have shaped my development over the years.

To the staff at Kingswood, who, despite my early disasters, not only did not walk out in disgust when I was made deputy head but gave me their unstinting support over the years.

To Dick Adams, principal of the two schools at Kingswood, who kept faith in me and, when I was in near total despair, had the vision to give me new and unique opportunities with the youth club. To take the risk of sanctioning a venture which was to be independent of school discipline and which he could only enter by invitation was a remarkable step.

I remember Bill Hall, head of the training school, with respect and affection, and not a little surprise that in spite of my Byron House schemozzle he did not veto my appointment as his deputy. I do have a clear recollection of our first detailed conversation after my appointment. It was to the effect that while he had always believed that I would make a good deputy, and eventually a noteworthy head, he thought my first promotion would have been still a few years away. Thank you, Bill, for overcoming your doubts and giving me the chance. We were a good team!

I did not always see eye to eye with John Briers, our clinical psychologist, but we operated with mutual respect. I learnt a great deal from him and in due course we produced a joint memorandum on the setting up of a therapeutic community within an approved school. We both moved on before it came to fruition but I took its principles with me to my eighteen years as head of a school for maladjusted boys.

Theo Griffiths came to Kingswood as teacher for the most retarded group, but very soon progressed to third-in-charge and later deputy head. We were not only fellow Methodists and good friends, but he had superb practical skills which I lacked. Indeed all our skills seemed complementary and we worked happily together for twenty-seven years. We remain in close contact.

To mention all the staff by name is unnecessary. I remember you all and give you thanks.

Turning to more contemporary debts of gratitude, I must offer thanks to Janet and Bernard, good friends from church who have read substantial extracts and made helpful comments to curb my wilder flights of fancy.

And finally thanks to my family, daughters and grandchildren who have given steady encouragement and support. To Lynn, who has typed most of the manuscript, coping magnificently with my longhand. To Tom, grandson and publisher, who assures me that he takes the book on its merits and not as a favour to the old grump. And to my daughters Kate and Chris, who have given me incisive and much appreciated criticism.

My greatest debt is to Joyce. We met in my callow youth, she was my one and only, and we had over sixty years of happiness together. In my blackest times she never wavered in her support, but she was a power in her own right. Above all she taught me that while order and discipline are good starting points the absolute essentials for the rehabilitation of tortured souls are acceptance and love. She had them both in full and overflowing measure and it is therefore small wonder that she is remembered with gratitude by generations of boys.

Printed in the United Kingdom
by Lightning Source UK Ltd.
124576UK00002B/64-198/A